THE BEGINNER'S
Knitting
MANUAL

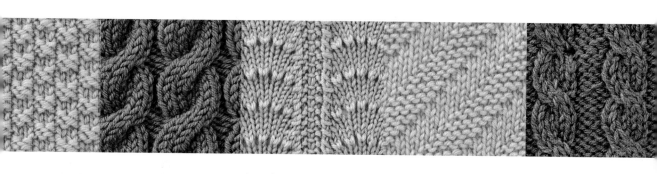

THE BEGINNER'S
Knitting
MANUAL

The Ultimate Book of Tips
and Techniques

Debbie Tomkies

Dover Publications, Inc.
Mineola, New York

The Beginner's Knitting Manual: The Ultimate Book of Tips and Techniques is a new work, first published by Dover Publications, Inc. in 2020.

International Standard Book Number

ISBN-13: 978-0-486-84288-2
ISBN-10: 0-486-84288-6

84288601

www.doverpublications.com

2 4 6 8 10 9 7 5 3 1

QUAR.329771

Conceived, edited, and designed by Quarto Publishing plc.
6 Blundell Street, London N7 9BH

Senior Editor: Ruth Patrick
Art Director: Gemma Wilson
Senior Art Editor: Emma Clayton
Designer: Joanna Bettles
Editorial Assistant: Charlene Fernandes
Photography: Nicki Dowey and Phil Wilkins
Illustrator: Kuo Kang Chen
Publisher: Samantha Warrington

Printed in Singapore by COS Printers

Contents

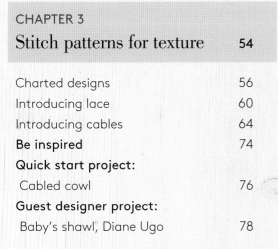

Welcome ...

I have been a passionate knitter since I was a child, learning from my granny when she came to visit from Scotland. As I got older I learned much through trial and error (quite a lot of error!), before landing my first job knitting brightly colored mohair sweaters (thank you, 1980s).

At university, knitting took a back seat until I started work. After a busy day, I rediscovered the benefits and therapeutic relaxation of picking up a pair of needles, a ball of squishy yarn, and a cup of tea.

My first break as a professional designer came when one of my designs was spotted by a knitting magazine editor. Four years later, I was designing each issue and writing step-by-step tutorials. Three books later and I'm now working for another knitting magazine, writing the knitters "agony aunt" column and the "how-to" features, answering questions from new and experienced knitters alike.

It is this experience that I hope to share in this, my fourth book. I want to give you all the skills you need to get started, master the essentials, and build your confidence to allow you to start your own knitting adventure.

To encourage you along the way, I've designed five lovely projects, building on the skills you will learn in each chapter. To further inspire you, I have asked five fabulous designers to share one of their favorite designs. I hope you will have as much pleasure knitting them as we have had designing them.

DEBBIE TOMKIES

About this book

This book explains all the core skills of knitting, from picking up a pair of needles to achieving a professional finish. There are also plenty of practice patterns for swatches and projects.

CHAPTERS 1–2
PAGES 8–53

The essential skills of knitting are explained here, from choosing yarn and needles to working the basic stitches, increasing and decreasing stitches to shape your work, and checking your gauge.

BE INSPIRED

Each chapter features a gallery of work from professional knitting designers, offering inspiration and information on how each piece was made.

CHAPTERS 3–6

PAGES 54–153

Once you know the basic stitches you can start to experiment, from working lace and cables to create beautiful texture in your knitting (chapter 3) to working in the round (chapter 4). Learn how to work stripes, Fair Isle, and intarsia (chapter 5), and finishing techniques to give your work a professional look (chapter 6).

Lists of ideas and solutions provide quick answers to common questions plus tips and tricks for getting the best from your knitting.

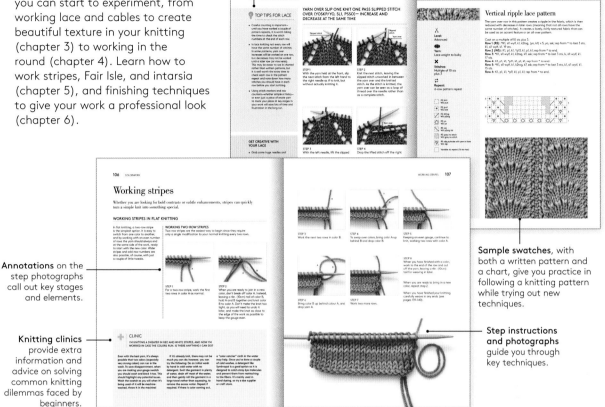

Annotations on the step photographs call out key stages and elements.

Knitting clinics provide extra information and advice on solving common knitting dilemmas faced by beginners.

Sample swatches, with both a written pattern and a chart, give you practice in following a knitting pattern while trying out new techniques.

Step instructions and photographs guide you through key techniques.

QUICK START AND GUEST DESIGNER PROJECTS

Test your new-found skills with the projects found toward the end of each chapter. The quick start projects (see right) are designed to get you off the mark quickly and efficiently. The guest designer projects show you how talented, professional knitting designers work, and provide you with an opportunity to take your skills to a higher level.

The techniques featured in the book are highlighted at the start of each project, so that you can refer to the relevant technique when making the project.

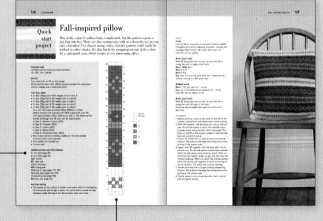

Knitting charts are provided to complement the written pattern, when it would be helpful to see a visual representation of the instructions.

1

GETTING STARTED

Getting started with knitting is not expensive—you can make many projects with just one pair of needles. There are yarns to suit all budgets and you needn't spend a lot for great results. Check out thrift stores, too, for repurposed needles and even yarns.

Needles

To begin your knitting journey, all you will need to get started is a pair of knitting needles, some yarn, a tape measure, and a pair of scissors. A suitable pair of knitting needles is your first requirement. Knitting needles are available in a wide range of materials, shapes, and sizes, from practical plastic or metal to wood, bamboo, and even glass. When it comes to choosing your first needles, try as many different types, lengths, shapes, and materials as you can.

NEEDLE TYPES

Remember that you may need at least two pairs of needles for your first project, so consider your budget when making your first purchase. If your budget limits you to buying inexpensive plastic or metal needles, that's fine; you will still be able to complete any knitting project. You can often pick up needles from charity stores or upcycling websites such as Freecycle or Craig's List.

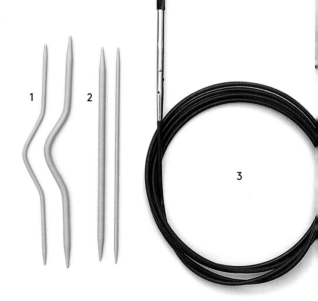

SINGLE-POINTED PAIRS OF NEEDLES
Widely available and commonly used, single-pointed needles are sold in pairs and have a point at one end and a knurl, knob, or other stopper at the other end to prevent the stitches sliding off. Use these needles for knitting flat fabrics.

DOUBLE-POINTED NEEDLES
These needles have points at both ends and are sold in sets of four or five needles. Often referred to as DPNs, they are used for knitting tubular fabrics such as socks, jumper sleeves, and seamless jumpers (also called knitting in the round). Extra-long DPNs can be used with a knitting belt or sheath for traditional Fair Isle knitting. DPNs can also be used for flat knitting and brioche, and for making i-cord (narrow tubes of knitting in the round normally used for edgings or bag straps).

CIRCULAR NEEDLES
A circular needle comprises two short, single-pointed needles, joined to each other by a flexible cord. The cord may be permanently attached, but there are also sets available with interchangeable needles (tips) and cords of different lengths. Circular needles are versatile because they can be used for knitting flat fabrics as an alternative to single-pointed needles, or for knitting tubular fabrics in place of DPNs.

CABLE NEEDLES
Also called cable pins, cable needles are short, double-pointed needles that are straight, hook-shaped, or with a kink in the middle. They are used when creating cables as a means of temporarily holding a small number of stitches. Choose a size that is the same as, or slightly smaller than, your main knitting to avoid stretching your cable stitches.

NEEDLE LENGTHS

The most common lengths for standard single-pointed needles are 12in. (30cm) and 14in. (35cm), and these will suit most knitters. For small projects (toys, accessories, etc.) and for knitting with children, shorter needles of around 6–8in. (15–20cm) are available.

5IN. (12.5CM), 7½IN. (19CM), AND 10IN. (25CM) DPNS

Choose the length you find most comfortable to work with, bearing in mind that the more stitches you have and the thicker the yarn, the longer your DPNs will likely need to be.

EXTRA-LONG, 16IN. (40CM) DPNS

Very long needles are used for some traditional Fair Isle techniques, where the needles are held in a leather belt or wooden sheath worn around the waist. This isn't a commonly used technique today but was once popular in Europe, and allows for fast knitting.

CIRCULAR NEEDLE TIPS AND CORDS

The tip of a circular needle refers to the actual needle; the cord joins the two needles together. Tips are normally short, around 4in. (10cm). Cords range from 8in. (20cm) to 60in. (150cm). The length of the cord should be chosen to give a circumference slightly smaller than that of the tube being knitted to allow the work to move easily round the circle without being stretched.

1 Cranked cable needles, 2 Straight cable needles, 3 Wood circular needle with plastic cord, 4 Bamboo single-pointed needles, 5 Wood double-pointed needles, 6 Bamboo double-pointed needles, 7 Square-shaped wooden circular needle tips, 8 Aluminum metal single-pointed needles.

NEEDLE SHAPES

ROUND

This is by far and away the most common needle shape on the market; it is easy to use and is available in all formats, sizes, and materials.

SQUARE

Many knitters with dexterity problems report that these needles are a much easier shape to grip and manipulate. So, they are worth a try if you find traditional round needles uncomfortable. Square needles are more expensive than round ones, but prices will no doubt become more competitive with time.

HEXAGONAL

These needles are at the upper end of the price scale but are pretty and comfortable to use. The shape also makes them less likely to roll off the table!

8

7

6

NEEDLE MATERIALS

PLASTIC NEEDLES

Plastic needles are inexpensive and are readily available in a wide range of sizes. Plastic needles are the first choice for many knitters, beginners and experienced alike. Flexible and light to use, you can buy a pair at a time or choose a pre-packaged set with a range of sizes.

BAMBOO

Bamboo needles are flexible, lightweight, and warm to the touch, making them popular with knitters who have arthritis or rheumatism. Budget bamboo needles can split with use, so buy the best pair within your budget. They can be lightly sanded with emery paper if they develop rough spots over time.

WOOD

There are many beautiful wooden needles on the market and many knitters find these the most comfortable to work with because they are warm, light, and easy on the hands. Like bamboo they can break, but can be sanded with care.

METAL

Many knitters prefer metal needles because they are virtually indestructible. They are the needles of choice for many lace knitters because they have the sharpest points for fine work. The smooth finish also makes them a popular choice for knitting at speed. Prices vary significantly for metal needles.

GLASS

Glass needles are a luxury choice: they are lovely to use and very beautiful. They are more durable than you may imagine since most are made from Pyrex, although naturally they are best kept away from the rough and tumble you may subject your normal needles to. Not as wide a range of sizes, particularly small sizes, but now available in single-pointed, double-pointed, and circular formats.

Your knit kit

In addition to your knitting needles, there are a few items that you will find very useful, and a small number that are essential. In the majority of cases, you will already have what you need at home. There are, of course, lots of gadgets and accessories that you may wish to purchase as you progress.

ESSENTIALS

PEN, PENCIL, AND NOTEPAPER

These essential knitting bag items are useful for marking off where you are in a pattern and making notes about patterns and any alterations you may have made. If you reach the stage where you are designing your own knits, jot down any thoughts, ideas, and inspiration for these and future projects.

KNITTING NEEDLE GAUGE

A good needle gauge will enable you to identify the size of any knitting needle and is useful for converting between different measurement systems (for example, metric and imperial). A gauge is also handy if you are given needles, or buy them secondhand, because the numbers may have worn away with use.

SCISSORS

Choose small scissors with sharp points because these will allow you to cut neatly and in the right place. It is worth investing in good-quality scissors, since inexpensive ones may snag your knitted fabric. Keep them in a pouch or case to prevent accidents.

YARN NEEDLES

Referred to variously as yarn needles, bodkins, and darning needles, you will need a small selection of these to sew up your knits. Blunt or round-ended needles are useful for sewing up seams where it is important not to split the yarn. Choose a size appropriate to the yarn.

SEWING OR TAPESTRY NEEDLES

Needles with sharper points, such as the type used for needlepoint or tapestry, are useful for sewing in ends where you need to split the yarn. Sewing needles can also be used for adding buttons, zippers, and other accessories. Select a size to suit your thickness of yarn. If you are planning to add beads, you will need a beading needle because even regular sewing needles are too thick for most beads.

TAPE MEASURE AND RULER

Use a tape measure for body measurements and for measuring anything that isn't flat. A ruler is useful

for measuring stitches and rows for gauge swatches. It also doubles as a handy marker for keeping your place on knitting charts.

CONTRASTING THREAD

You will find that $\frac{1}{2}$oz (10g) or so of smooth thread (cotton is a good choice) in a contrasting color to your knitting will have many uses. For example, it is useful for holding stitches, marking key stages in your knitting, indicating the location of pattern repeats, and for specific techniques, such as provisional cast on and lifelines.

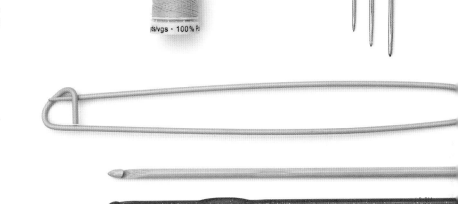

PINS

Pins are used to hold your knitting together when assembling. Choose large-headed pins where possible so that you can see them easily. A selection of longer pins for longer seams and shorter pins for smaller areas will be useful. Special T-pins are available for blocking knits. These have a T-shaped head, making them easier and safer to use vertically (as opposed to flat to the knitting).

OPTIONAL EXTRAS

STITCH HOLDERS

Available in several lengths to accommodate different numbers of stitches, stitch holders look like large safety pins. A safety pin can be used for a small number of stitches, but be careful not to snag the yarn on the hinge.

ROW COUNTERS

Pen and paper are perfectly adequate for recording your knitting progress, but there are also lots of handy row counters on the market. These range from simple plastic click mechanisms and barrels that sit on the end of your needles, to apps to download onto your smartphone.

STITCH MARKERS

Ranging from inexpensive plastic to beautiful, handmade beaded sets, stitch markers denote key points in your knitting; for example, marking the end of a round or pattern repeat. Choose a size slightly larger than your needles, checking that they slide easily and that any beads won't catch in your work.

SPLIT RING AND CLIP-IN MARKERS

These are similar to stitch markers but with an open end, allowing them to be inserted and removed anywhere at any time. Useful for marking key points in your work when you need to leave the marker in the work and return to it later.

POINT PROTECTORS

Flexible plastic or rubberized point protectors keep your work on the needles when you are not knitting. They also prevent points from poking out of workbags and prevent damage to the points of the needles.

CROCHET HOOKS

A selection of crochet hooks will come in handy for adding edgings and beads, and for picking up dropped stitches.

BOBBINS

Used in place of hand-wound "butterflies" to hold small amounts of yarn, usually for intarsia or Fair Isle work.

Yarn

Knitters around the globe may share a love of knitting, but they
have many and varied ways of describing the yarns they work with.

It is really more correct to use the term "yarn" to describe all the different types of "string" we knit with. Of course, "wool" is a term many knitters associate with any type of knitting yarn, regardless of the fiber from which it is made. Strictly speaking, however, the term "wool" only applies when the actual fiber content of the yarn is processed sheep's fleece. It is therefore more correct to use the term "yarn" to separate it from the idea of fiber content, which describes the raw material, or materials, from which a yarn is made.

A further aspect of any yarn description is its quality. This may be described in different ways, depending on the country of origin of the yarn (or indeed of the pattern or the designer). In this context, quality doesn't usually refer to how good the yarn is—that would generate a lengthy debate among any group of knitters!

YARN GLOSSARY

There are myriad technical words in the world of yarn. Here's a rundown of some of the key terms and their meaning in the context of knitting.

YARN
The basic material used to create a knitted fabric. This includes the many commercially produced yarns available from yarn stores and other shops, but also handspun or handmade yarns, and yarns made from wire, plastic, strips of fabric, or other materials.

FIBER CONTENT
Yarn fiber could come from an animal (for example, sheep, alpaca, camel, goat), from a plant (for example, cotton, hemp, linen, nettle, bamboo, soy), or from a man-made source (for example, acrylic, polyamide, wire, plastic). Regenerated fibers such as viscose, tencel, and rayon are made from wood pulp. Recycled fibers may include fabric or even plastic bottles. The choice of fiber content will influence the use, handle, appearance, and suitability of a yarn for a particular project.

YARN QUALITY
A broad term used to describe the nature of the yarn. This will often incorporate, among other things, yarn weight, yardage, how many plies the yarn has, and yarn count.

WEIGHT
In the context of yarn quality, weight refers to the thickness of the yarn, not the actual weight of the ball/skein. Terms to describe yarn weight vary and there is some overlap with plies and yarn count. US terminology, for example, may include fingering, sport, worsted, and bulky. Equivalent UK terms refer to the thickness of a yarn by ply—2-ply, 4-ply, and so on.

PLIES
This refers to the way a yarn is made. Yarn starts out life as one strand, referred to as a singles thread or singles. It is then plied (either by twisting or by folding) with one or more other threads to create a thicker yarn. A 2-ply yarn is made from two strands, a 4-ply from four strands, and so on. Depending on the thickness of the original strand, this determines the thickness of the finished yarn and therefore its quality. Traditionally, in the UK, a 2-ply would describe a lace weight (fine) yarn but if the yarn begins life as a single, thick strand, a 2-ply of this yarn could be much thicker, so using plies to describe yarn thickness can be misleading.

YARDAGE/METERAGE
This is a useful guide when deciding the amount of yarn needed for a project. Some fibers are heavier than others, so there are fewer yards per ounce (meters per gram) with, for example, a silk than a cashmere yarn. However, 100yd (92m) of fingering quality silk should knit the same number of stitches as 100yd (92m) of fingering quality cashmere, making this a useful measure when substituting yarns.

YARN COUNT
The yarn count is the number of yards of yarn in a given weight (actual weight) of finished yarn. Rather unhelpfully there are many systems for arriving at a yarn count, including worsted count, linen count, cotton count, Yorkshire count, and tex. Yarn count isn't something most knitters will need to know to get started or buy yarn for a project.

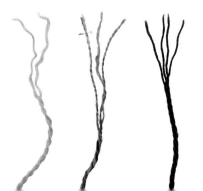

CHOOSING AND SUBSTITUTING YARN

At some time, most knitters will find the perfect pattern only to discover that the recommended yarn has been discontinued, or is one that they don't like or can't wear due to allergies. Other times, a great pattern can be made even better by incorporating a small amount of a luxury or novelty yarn, or an expensive yarn can be substituted with a more economical choice. Although this may seem a little daunting, substituting yarns is quite straightforward and can be great fun, too. Yarn substitutions fall broadly into three categories:

1 LIKE FOR LIKE

If a pattern calls for a pure wool yarn in a fingering weight but you can't buy the stated yarn, you need to replace it with a yarn that is as similar in weight and quality as possible. You can often find this information on the ball band. Look for the yards per ounce and the needle size/s. The chart on page 16 is a useful starting point for identifying yarn weights and types.

If you have a mystery yarn without a label, you can make an initial guess at its suitability for your project, without knitting a stitch, by checking the wraps per inch. You can work out the WPI by taking a straight ruler and wrapping the yarn around it until it covers an inch (don't wrap too tightly or you may distort the result). Compare your result to the chart on page 16. If the yarns are similar, it's worth pressing on with a gauge swatch.

2 ALL CHANGE

It may be necessary to change a yarn completely; for example, substituting a cotton yarn for wool if you have allergies. If this is the case, you will need to knit a gauge swatch. It's also a good idea to make it a bit larger than normal (double the size if possible). This is because the drape and handle of the fabrics can differ significantly. Consider the purpose, too. Wool is warm and great for sweaters. Cotton is much cooler and often reserved for summer wear. Swapping a superwash wool for a non-superwash one may seem simple, but bear in mind that the non-superwash will need handwashing, which is not ideal for, say, a busy parent or a garment that will need regular washing.

A complete change is the most challenging substitution, but by following these top tips it can be achieved successfully and with fantastic results.

3 SPICING IT UP

A plain pattern can often be enhanced, or a vintage pattern updated and customized, by including a small amount of a different yarn. If you have a thin yarn in the right fiber, you may be able to use two (or more) strands together. A 4-ply used with two strands is roughly equal to a DK yarn, for example. For two strands, test the wraps per inch as above, bearing in mind that the number of wraps should be divided by two, then compare to the desired yarn weight on the chart.

SHOPPING FOR YARN

If you are buying yarn to match a pattern, it may not be possible to make gauge squares. Fortunately, most ball bands should give details equivalent to a gauge square, showing the stitches/rows to the inch/centimeter usually worked in stockinette stitch and using a specified needle size. There may also be a recommended range of needle sizes for the yarn. While not as accurate as producing your own gauge squares, using a yarn that has a range of needle sizes and a gauge measurement close to that stated in your pattern should give a good gauge match.

Yarn name

Length and weight

Care instructions

Shade dye and lot numbers

Fiber content

Recommended knitting gauge

Recommended needle size(s) for stockinette stitch

DYELOTS

Yarn is spun in batches. Although manufacturers use consistent methods, there can still be slight differences between each batch. In knitting, this is referred to as the "dye batch" or "dyelot." When you are buying yarn, the store should make sure all the yarn is from the same dyelot, but it's worth checking, especially if you're buying online. Differences in dyelots may seem small but can be surprisingly visible when knitted up.

USING YOUR STASH

If you want to use up existing yarn from your stash, or use handspun yarn for a particular project, you may not be able to work out if your yarn will be suitable. In this case, follow the instructions below.

Begin by choosing a yarn that looks similar to the pattern yarn. Wrap the yarn closely around a ruler until 1in. (2.5cm) has been covered. Count how many times the yarn is wrapped around the ruler to give you the wraps per inch (WPI). Use the chart below to decide the closest yarn type to your yarn. If this is the same as the pattern yarn, you are well on the way. If not, you may have to consider using a different yarn.

YARN WEIGHT SYMBOL AND CATEGORY NAMES	0 Lace	1 Super fine	2 Fine	3 Light	4 Medium	5 Bulky	6 Super bulky
Types of yarns in category	Fingering 10-count crochet thread	Sock, fingering, baby	Sport, baby	DK, light worsted	Worsted, Afghan, Aran	Chunky, craft, rug	Bulky, roving
Knit gauge range in stockinette stitch to 4in. (10cm)	33–40 sts	27–32 sts	23–26 sts	21–24 sts	16–20 sts	12–15 sts	6–11 sts
Recommended needle in US-size range	000–1	1–3	3–5	5–7	7–9	9–11	11 and larger
Recommended needle in metric-size range	1.5–2.25mm	2.25–3.25mm	3.25–3.75mm	3.75–4.5mm	4.5–5.5mm	5.5–8mm	8mm and larger
Wraps per inch (WPI)	16–18 WPI	14 WPI	12 WPI	11 WPI	8–9 WPI	7 WPI	6 or fewer WPI

1 Organic wool,
2 Recycled, 3 Bamboo,
4 Acrylic, 5 Organic
cotton, 6 Silk, 7 Cotton,
8 Alpaca, 9 Merino.

1

2

3

4

5

6

7

8

9

How to read knitting patterns

Knitting patterns may look complicated and intimidating, but once you get to grips with the basic structure, following a pattern is no more difficult than cooking with a recipe. Always read the pattern through before beginning a project and, as a general rule, knit the pieces in the order presented in the pattern, since there may be a specific reason for doing so.

SIZING (1)
A pattern will normally begin with sizing and will usually provide two distinct measurements: one is "actual size," the other the "to fit" measurement.

Actual size refers to the physical dimensions of the garment when it is knitted and will include extra inches (centimeters) to allow for "ease." The amount of ease will vary depending on the garment's intended fit. A skinny jumper, for example, will have less ease than a long jacket.

Because it can be difficult to know how much ease is built into a garment, pattern writers will also provide a "to fit" measurement. This refers to the body measurements of the wearer. Several measurements may be given, for example, sleeve length and length of neck to shoulder, but, because these measurements can be adjusted during knitting, it is best to select your size based on the "to fit" chest measurement.

SCHEMATIC
A schematic is an outline drawing showing where key measurements should be taken. This is particularly useful for garments such as hats, or garments with unusual features such as dropped waistlines, where it is important to measure at the right place to achieve the desired finished size.

MATERIALS AND EQUIPMENT (2)
Here you will find essential information about the yarn used to knit the pattern, plus details of any additional items you may need, such as zippers and buttons. The needles used for the project will also be listed, but bear in mind that you may need to change these depending on your gauge.

For best results it is advisable to use the yarn stated in the pattern. If you intend to substitute for an alternative

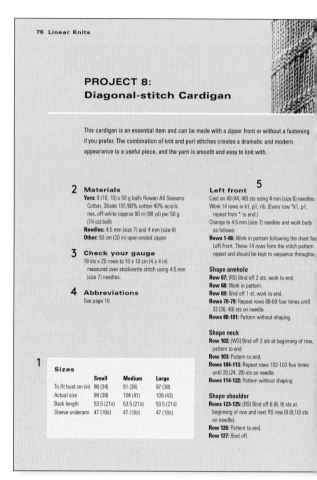

76 Linear Knits

PROJECT 8:
Diagonal-stitch Cardigan

This cardigan is an essential item and can be made with a zipper front or without a fastening if you prefer. The combination of knit and purl stitches creates a dramatic and modern appearance to a useful piece, and the yarn is smooth and easy to knit with.

2   Materials
Yarn: 9 (10, 10) x 50 g balls Rowan All Seasons Cotton, Shade 191/60% cotton:40% acrylic mix, off-white (approx 90 m (98 yd) per 50 g (1¾ oz) ball)
Needles: 4.5 mm (size 7) and 4 mm (size 6)
Other: 50 cm (20 in) open-ended zipper

3   Check your gauge
18 sts x 25 rows to 10 x 10 cm (4 x 4 in) measured over stockinette stitch using 4.5 mm (size 7) needles.

4   Abbreviations
See page 16.

5
Left front
Cast on 40 (44, 48) sts using 4 mm (size 6) needles. Work 14 rows in k1, p1, rib. (Every row *k1, repeat from * to end.)
Change to 4.5 mm (size 7) needles and work body as follows:
Rows 1-66: Work in pattern following the chart for Left Front. These 14 rows form the stitch pattern repeat and should be kept to sequence throughout.

Shape armhole
Row 67: (RS) Bind off 2 sts, work to end.
Row 68: Work in pattern.
Row 69: Bind off 1 st, work to end.
Rows 70-79: Repeat rows 68-69 four times until 32 (36, 40) sts on needle.
Rows 80-101: Pattern without shaping.

Shape neck
Row 102: (WS) Bind off 2 sts at beginning of row, pattern to end
Row 103: Pattern to end.
Rows 104-113: Repeat rows 102-103 five times until 20 (24, 28) sts on needle.
Rows 114-122: Pattern without shaping.

Shape shoulder
Rows 123-125: (RS) Bind off 6 (8, 9) sts at beginning of row and next RS row (8 (8,10) sts on needle).
Row 126: Pattern to end.
Row 127: Bind off.

1

Sizes	Small	Medium	Large
To.fit bust cm (in)	86 (34)	91 (36)	97 (38)
Actual size	99 (39)	104 (41)	109 (43)
Back length	53.5 (21¼)	53.5 (21¼)	53.5 (21¼)
Sleeve underarm	47 (18¾)	47 (18¾)	47 (18¾)

yarn, see pages 15–16. When buying yarn, make sure to buy enough to complete the garment and check it is all from the same dyelot (see page 15).

GAUGE (3)
Gauge, also referred to as tension, is a crucial part of any pattern. Correct gauge is the key to making a garment that fits as the designer intended. See page 46 for instructions on checking your gauge.

ABBREVIATIONS (4)
To make sure that patterns are easy to follow (and also a manageable size for printing), pattern writers use certain conventions and abbreviations. Many of these will take a similar format, but each pattern will have a section that covers any abbreviations used and will detail any special instructions unique to that particular design. It is worthwhile reading through the pattern and any abbreviations or special notes before starting, even if

on the size of the garment. For example, "cast on 100 (120, 140, 180)" means that if you are making the first size you cast on 100 stitches, the second size cast on 120, the third 140, and so on. It's helpful to photocopy the pattern and mark the relevant numbers/instructions for your size. If the instructions only give one number, this number is used for all sizes.

Parentheses may also be used to indicate sections where the instructions are to be repeated a number of times. For example, "k1, (p1, k3) 3 times" means k1, p1, k3, p1, k3, p1, k3.

ASTERISKS (6)

Asterisks are used in a similar way to parentheses to indicate sections of a pattern that are to be repeated. These can be repeats within a row, a repeat of several rows, or even a repeat of a large section of a garment. For example, "k1,*p1, k3, rep from * to last st, k1" means k1, p1, k3, then repeat just the p1, k3 as many times as required until you reach the last stitch of the row. The last stitch is then knitted. This can also be described as "k1, *p1, k3*, rep from * to * to last st, k1" and means that you should repeat the section between the two asterisks.

Where a pattern has two parts that are similar—for example, a jumper back and front—the pattern may say "FRONT: Work as for back until **." The front is knitted in the same way as the back until the double asterisk shown on the back section is reached.

Watch for multiple asterisks and make sure to work to the correct number of asterisks. If you see what appears to be a stray asterisk, it will become relevant later in the pattern.

Asterisks and parentheses may be used in the same line of a pattern. So, "*k1, (p1, k3) 3 times from * to end" means k1, p1, k3, p1, k3, p1, k3, then repeat k1, p1, k3, p1, k3, p1, k3 until the end of the row. Different shaped parentheses, for example [ ] or ( ), may also be used in combination. Treat matching parentheses as a pair, working the stitches within the matching pair as with asterisk/parentheses combinations.

you are a seasoned knitter. This is particularly important when using patterns that have been translated because terminology can differ between countries.

ASSEMBLY

Also referred to as making up, this part of the pattern explains how to prepare pieces for sewing up (for example, whether to block the pieces, pin them, etc.) and how to sew the various parts together. It is advisable to follow the order given. This is because some patterns will ask you to sew up certain seams (for example, one shoulder seam), then do something else such as add a neckband, before going on to sew up other seams. Depending on the pattern, you may be advised to use a certain stitch or technique. If not, refer to pages 138–140 for suggestions.

PARENTHESES: SIZING (5)

Parentheses can be used to indicate points in a pattern where you are required to do different things depending

2

ESSENTIALS STITCHES AND TECHNIQUES

Learning to knit is satisfying, fun, and relaxing. You'll be amazed at how much you can achieve by following the basic techniques in this chapter. By using just two simple stitches you can make a huge variety of beautiful knits.

Holding the needles

There are numerous ways to hold your needles and there is really no "wrong" way if it allows you to make a nice, neat knit fabric comfortably and enjoyably. Here are some suggestions to get you started.

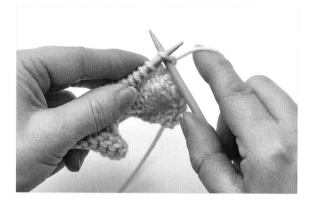

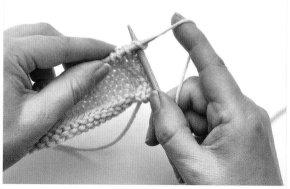

KNIFE AND FORK METHOD

Hold the needles as you would hold a knife and fork, with your hands over the top of each needle. This knitting style is quick and efficient, the fabric doesn't bunch up, and the thumb doesn't poke into and distort the work. It is suitable for both flat knitting and knitting in the round.

CURLED METHOD

This method is similar to the knife and fork method, but the hands are more curled around and below the needles. This can give more support to the needles and may be more comfortable on the wrists. This method is also suitable for flat knitting and knitting in the round.

PEN METHOD

Hold the left needle like a knife and the right needle like a pen. This style may be slower than the other styles as the work can become scrunched up between the crook of the thumb/index finger and the needle tip.

 CLINIC

I'VE SEEN PICTURES OF KNITTERS TUCKING THE RIGHT-HAND NEEDLE UNDER THEIR ARMPIT. IS THIS A GOOD IDEA?

This can be a quick method as the right hand has more freedom to move using small, efficient motions. However, tucking is not suitable for knitting on circular needles or short double-pointed needles. For this reason, knitters who normally tuck but want to knit in the round may need to adapt their needle and yarn-holding style to accommodate knitting on short, unsupported needles.

Holding the yarn

As with holding the needles, there is no right or wrong way to hold your yarn—do whatever works for you.

HOLDING THE YARN IN THE RIGHT HAND

This method is suitable for all needle positions and knitting styles. The yarn may be wrapped around the fingers in a variety of ways.

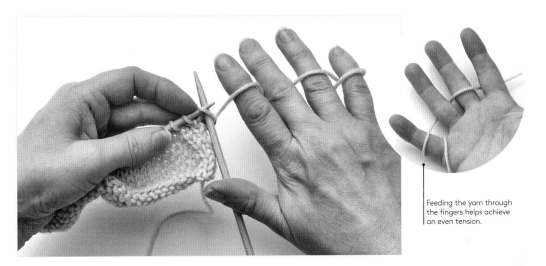

Feeding the yarn through the fingers helps achieve an even tension.

HOLDING THE YARN IN THE LEFT HAND

Believed to have originated in Germany and often referred to as "continental knitting," this method is suitable for all knitting styles and needle positions, although is arguably easier with the curled or knife and fork method.

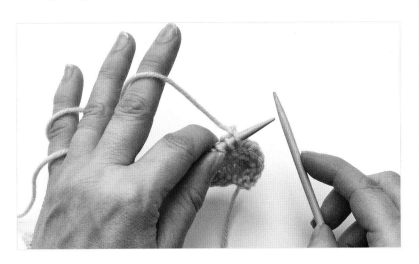

TOP TIPS FOR HOLDING THE YARN

- It is useful to practice several techniques and ways to wrap the yarn around your fingers, since this will enable you to vary your style, giving your muscles and arms a rest.

- The ability to use both the left and right hands to hold the yarn is invaluable when knitting colorwork, as one hand can hold each color without the irritation of untangling yarns every row.

Making a slip knot

The slip knot forms the first stitch and is used to begin
most cast ons.

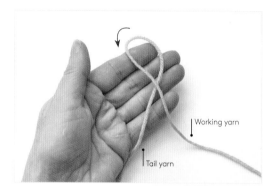

STEP 1
Take the working yarn over the tail yarn to
make a circle.

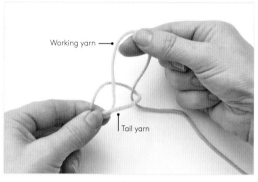

STEP 2
Hold the circle of yarn firmly in either your left or
right hand. Use the other thumb and first finger
to dip into the circle and pull the tail yarn back
toward you, through the circle. Be careful not to
pull the tail completely through the circle.

STEP 3
Keep hold of the loop in one hand and the two
ends of yarn in the other and gently draw the loop
away from the two ends of yarn until a knot begins
to form.

STEP 4
Tighten the knot and draw it up onto the needle.
The loop should be snug but not too tight because
you will need to be able to insert the needle
through it.

Casting on

Casting on marks the beginning of the knitting process and provides the basis for the initial stitches from which your knit fabric will be formed. Choosing the right method for casting on will give your knits a professional look and ensure that they stand up to wear and tear without losing their shape.

TWO-NEEDLE CAST ON

The two-needle cast on produces a nice, firm edge. It isn't particularly stretchy but holds its shape well, making it a good choice for edgings, scarves, wraps, and garments where the cast on isn't followed by ribbing.

STEP 1
Make a slip knot, leaving a tail around 6in. (15cm) long. Place it snugly on the left needle, and hold the tail yarn evenly tensioned around the fingers of your right hand (UK style) or left hand (continental style).

STEP 2
Insert the tip of the right needle from front to back into the front of the slip knot.

STEP 3
Wrap the working yarn around the right needle by bringing it up under the needle from right to left, taking it between the two needles, over the top of the needle and holding it to the right.

STEP 4
Maintaining an even tension on the working yarn, use the right needle to draw the working loop between the needles. Opening out your hands and elbows as though opening a pair of shears will help you to see the working yarn and make drawing the loop through easier.

STEP 5
Insert the tip of the left needle from front to back into the loop on the right needle. Slide the loop onto the left needle and draw the stitch up so it is snug, but not too tight. The slip knot counts as one stitch, so you now have two stitches cast on.

How the finished cast on should look.

LONG-TAIL CAST ON (CONTINENTAL)

This cast on is a little more difficult to master than the two-needle cast on, but it does give a nice, elastic edge. This makes it a good choice where some stretch in the cast on is required, such as with sock cuffs.

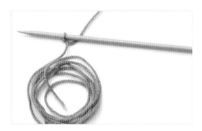

STEP 1
Estimate the length of yarn needed for the cast-on stitches. This is usually approximately three times the length of the cast-on edge. Make a slip knot at this point and place it on the right needle.

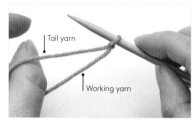

STEP 2
Hold both the working yarn and the tail yarn in the left hand, with the working yarn to the back and the tail yarn closest to you.

STEP 3
Keeping both strands tensioned, insert the thumb and first finger of the left hand down between the two strands. Hold the strands apart in a V-shape with the finger and thumb pointing down.

STEP 4
Keeping the yarn tension even, tilt the left thumb toward you.

STEP 5
Insert the right needle from left to right below the strand of yarn at the front of the thumb, bringing the first finger up as you do so. Take the right needle away from you over the loop on the first finger. The working yarn will be looped over the right needle.

STEP 6
Take the needle over both the strand of yarn you can see between the thumb and first finger (the tail) and the strand laying over the first finger (the working yarn).

STEP 7
Bring the needle toward you, taking it through the loop of yarn wrapped around the thumb (the tail yarn).

STEP 8
Take the thumb away from you and lift the loop on the thumb over the right needle.

STEP 9
Slide the thumb out of the loop and draw up snugly on the right needle.

STEP 10
Two stitches cast on (the slip knot counts as the first stitch). Repeat steps 1–9 until the desired number of stitches have been cast on.

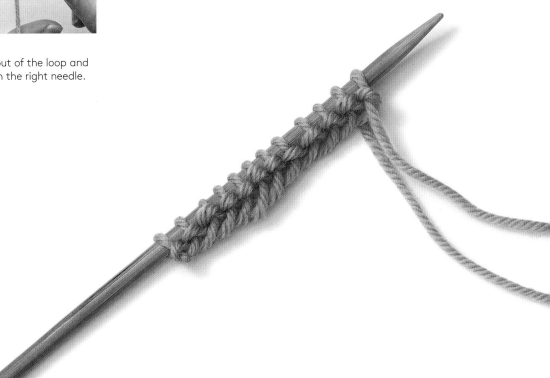

The knit stitch

The knit stitch forms the basis of many of the more complex knitting stitches and patterns, and is a fundamental part of many techniques. It is the first stitch that most knitters learn and once you have mastered it, a whole world of patterns and projects opens up to you.

WORKING YARN IN THE RIGHT HAND

STEP 1
With the yarn held in the right hand, insert the tip of the right needle from left to right into the front of the first stitch on the left needle. The right needle goes beneath the left needle with the tip pointing away from you.

STEP 2
Use the right hand to bring up the working yarn from right to left (counterclockwise) beneath the right needle. Bring the yarn toward you and take from left to right over the right needle. Keep the yarn lightly tensioned but do not hold too tightly.

STEP 3
Maintaining a light tension on the working yarn, open out the hands slightly as though opening a pair of shears. You should see a small opening in the work with the wrapped right needle behind. Keeping the left needle steady, angle the right needle and bring the tip toward you through the opening.

💡 TOP TIPS FOR YARN IN THE RIGHT HAND

- Try to keep the working yarn close and parallel to the right needle. This will help prevent it from slipping off the needle as you bring the right needle through the opening.

- If you're struggling to make your stitches, try holding the yarn and needles differently.

- Don't worry if the first row feels quite tight. As you practice, your gauge will become easier and more even.

STEP 4
With the tip of the right needle now in front of the left needle, you should see a loop of yarn on the left needle behind the right-hand tip. Keeping the working yarn to the right, carefully slide this loop of yarn off the left needle.

STEP 5
Your first knit stitch is now complete and is sitting on the right needle with the working yarn attached. Draw up the working yarn so that the stitches are even, not too tight or floppy. Note that the stitch is smooth on the front of the work with a bump on the back. Repeat these steps until all the stitches on the left needle have been worked (unless the pattern directs otherwise).

WORKING YARN IN THE LEFT HAND (CONTINENTAL)

STEP 1
Hold the working yarn in the left hand behind the left needle.

STEP 2
Insert the tip of the right needle into the front of the first stitch on the left needle. The right needle goes into the stitch from left to right.

STEP 3
Tensioning the yarn a little with the left hand, take the yarn around the tip of the right needle.

STEP 4
Use the tip of the right needle to "scoop" the working yarn through the stitch on the left needle to the front of the work. You should now have a loop on the front (right needle) and one on the back (left needle).

FACTS ABOUT THE KNIT STITCH

1 You may hear knitters talking about "garter stitch." Garter stitch (sometimes also called "plain knitting" in older patterns) is simply a pattern where every stitch and every row is made using the knit stitch.

2 Garter stitch creates an attractive fabric with a springy, ridged appearance. It is a reversible fabric, making it useful for items where both sides may be visible.

3 When working the knit stitch, the stitch is smooth as it faces you. On the reverse, the same stitch has a bump or ridge. Knitting every row creates alternating rows of smooth troughs and bumpy ridges and a bouncy, ridged fabric.

4 Garter stitch is one of the few stitch patterns that gives a square fabric—each stitch has the same height and width. So, a fabric that is 20 stitches wide and 20 rows tall should be square.

TOP TIPS FOR YARN IN THE LEFT HAND

- If you're struggling to keep the yarn on the needles, try controlling the yarn by holding it over the left middle finger rather than the first finger (or vice versa).

- Adjusting the angle of your needles will help make your knitting easier if it feels tight or awkward.

- Take regular breaks, especially when you're learning, to avoid building tension in your neck, hands, and shoulders.

STEP 5
Carefully allow the loop on the left needle to drop off. One stitch is now completed. Repeat these steps until all the stitches on the left needle have been worked (unless the pattern directs otherwise).

The purl stitch

The purl stitch is the second stitch that all knitters need in their repertoire. Armed with this stitch and the knit stitch, a vast range of patterns and design opportunities opens up to even a novice knitter.

3 USEFUL THINGS TO KNOW ABOUT THE PURL STITCH

- Simply combining knit and purl stitches makes it possible to produce an extensive range of beautiful, textured patterns.

- Alternating knit and purl stitches are the basis of most rib stitches.

- Purl stitches can be identified because they have the bump at the front of the work facing you. The smooth side faces away from you.

WORKING YARN IN THE RIGHT HAND

STEP 1
Hold the working yarn in the right hand in front of the right needle so that it lays over the top of the needle from left to right.

STEP 2
Insert the tip of the right needle from right to left up into the front of the first stitch on the left needle. Keep the working yarn to the front of the work in your right hand.

STEP 3
Wrap the working yarn under and around the tip of the right needle going from right to left (counterclockwise). Tension the yarn slightly and hold it at a slight angle to the left of the right needle.

STEP 4
Pivot the right needle and take it back away from you, taking it through the loop that you should be able to see between the needles.

Loop of yarn

STEP 5
Bring the tip of the right needle out behind the left needle. There should be the loop of the working yarn on the right needle at the back and the yarn from the stitch at the front on the left needle.

STEP 6
Carefully slip the left needle out of the loop. One purl stitch is complete. To continue in purl, keep the yarn to the front of the work and repeat these steps to the end of the row (unless the pattern directs otherwise).

WORKING YARN IN THE LEFT HAND (CONTINENTAL)

STEP 1
Hold the working yarn in the left hand in front of the right needle so that it lays over the top of the needle from left to right.

STEP 2
Insert the tip of the right needle from right to left up into the front of the first stitch on the left needle. Wrap the working yarn under and around the tip of the right needle from right to left (counterclockwise). Tension the yarn slightly with your middle finger.

STEP 3
Use the first finger to bring the yarn forward, holding it parallel and close to the right needle.

STEP 4
Carefully lift the left needle over the right needle and take the tip of the right needle out behind the left needle.

STEP 5
There should be the loop of the working yarn on the right needle at the back and the yarn from the stitch at the front on the left needle.

STEP 6
Carefully slip the left needle out of the loop. One purl stitch is complete. Repeat these steps to the end of the row (unless the pattern directs otherwise).

 ## WHAT IS STOCKING STITCH? IS IT THE SAME AS STOCKINETTE?

"Stockinette" and "stocking" stitch describe the familiar, smooth-faced fabric that is a mainstay of many knit garments.

To create a stockinette-stitch fabric, all the smooth faces of all the stitches must be on the same side of the knitting. To do this, it is necessary to introduce a stitch that has the opposite characteristics to the knit stitch, i.e. bumpy on the facing side, smooth on the reverse. This role is fulfilled by the purl stitch. By working in alternating rows of purl and knit stitches, it is then possible to create a fabric that is smooth on one side, with all the ridges together on the reverse.

FRONT

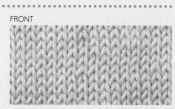

BACK

Level:
Beginner

Yarn:
Lace weight to super bulky

Stitches:
Multiple of 4 sts

Repeat:
4-row pattern repeat

RS: knit
WS: purl

RS: purl
WS: knit

4-stitch repeat

Double seed stitch

A straightforward pattern of small knit and purl blocks, worked in pairs to give a checkerboard effect.

Cast on a multiple of 4 sts.
Row 1 (RS): * k2, p2; repeat from * to end.
Row 2 (WS): * k2, p2; repeat from * to end.
Row 3 (RS): * p2, k2; repeat from * to end.
Row 4 (WS): * p2, k2; repeat from * to end.

Level:
Beginner

Yarn:
Lace weight to bulky

Stitches:
Multiple of 8 sts

Repeat:
16-row pattern repeat

☐ RS: knit
   WS: purl

☉ RS: purl
   WS: knit

☐ 8-stitch repeat

Garter diagonals

This simple pattern works well as an all-over pattern. It could be mirrored to produce an interesting, large chevron, perhaps down the back of a cardigan or jacket. It is suited to a wide range of yarn weights—to get the most from the pattern, choose a yarn with good stitch definition.

Cast on a multiple of 8 sts.
Row 1 and all odd-numbered rows (RS): k.
Row 2 (WS): * k5, p3; repeat from * to end.
Row 4 (WS): * p1, k5, p2; repeat from * to end.
Row 6 (WS): * p2, k5, p1; repeat from * to end.
Row 8 (WS): * p3, k5; repeat from * to end.
Row 10 (WS): * k1, p3, k4; repeat from * to end.
Row 12 (WS): * k2, p3, k3; repeat from * to end.
Row 14 (WS): * k3, p3, k2; repeat from * to end.
Row 16 (WS): * k4, p3, k1; repeat from * to end.
Repeat rows 1–16, finish with rows 1–2.

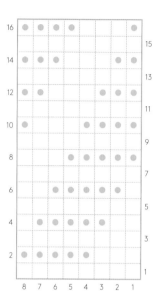

Increasing

Increases may be used to add shape, contour, and structure to knits. Curves, pleats, darts, edgings, or decorative stitches may all involve increases in one form or another.

Knit fabrics can be shaped in different ways:

- Using different needle sizes
- Choosing different stitch patterns
- Creating extra stitches at strategic points in the work

Increases may be made individually with single stitches, or with a number of stitches at once. Extra stitches may also be cast on, for example, with buttonholes. Increases also play a vital part in the creation of many decorative stitches. Lace in particular relies on increases to create the delicate patterns of holes and eyelets.

There are various ways an increase can be worked and this can seem confusing, particularly to the beginner. It is useful to know, therefore, that most increases are based on four simple stitches and, once these have been mastered, any new stitch can be tackled with confidence. Increase stitches fall into four broad categories:

- Bar increase (see right)
- Lifted increase (see page 36)
- Raised increase (see page 37)
- Yarn over increase (see page 39)

BAR INCREASE

The term "bar increase" comes from the bump that can be seen at the front of the work when knitting or purling twice into the same stitch. This increase is easy to work and doesn't leave a hole or loose stitch. However, the bar is visible, so if you need an invisible increase, the lifted increase (see page 36) may be a better choice. Used decoratively, two bar increases can be paired around a central stitch or used to highlight an area of shaping, such as a raglan sleeve.

KNIT BAR INCREASE (KFB, KF & B, KTW)

STEP 1
Knit into the front of the stitch in the normal way.

STEP 2
Without dropping the stitch from the left needle, lift the right needle over from front to back and knit again into the back of the same stitch.

STEP 3
Slip the left needle carefully out of the loops to leave two stitches on the right needle.

PURLED BAR INCREASE (PFB, PF & B, PTW)

STEP 1
With the yarn held to the front as normal for a purl stitch, insert the tip of the right needle into the back of the next stitch by bringing the right needle from back to front through the back of the stitch.

STEP 2
Without allowing the loop on the left needle to drop off, purl this stitch as normal, taking the right needle out to the back of the work, but keeping the loop on the right needle in place. Don't allow the loop to drop off at this stage.

STEP 3
Keeping the yarn to the front, bring the right needle in front of the left and purl into the front of the same stitch. Allow the stitch to drop off the needle.

STEP 4
Remove the left needle and note that there is now an extra stitch, made by working twice into a single stitch.

TOP TIPS FOR THE PERFECT INCREASE

- If the designer specifies a particular way to increase in the pattern, follow the suggested method. If no method is specified, choose the least visible one.

- Be careful not to split the yarn, particularly when working twice into the same stitch.

- Vintage patterns may simply say "increase x stitches evenly across the row." Use graph paper to plot where to put your increases—it saves time and headaches in the long run!

CLINIC

CAN I SIMPLY CHANGE MY NEEDLES TO MAKE MY WORK BIGGER?

Using larger needles does increase the size of the knit fabric. Indeed, it is sometimes necessary to go up a needle size in order to match the gauge stated in a pattern.

However, this can also affect the feel, density, and drape of the work. This is because the whole of the stitch increases in size when a larger needle is used. Although this may not be very noticeable if the increase is just one needle size, going up more than two needle sizes is likely to make the stitches too open and the work loose and floppy. To achieve an increase in a specific area—for example, widening a sleeve from the narrow cuff to the much wider armhole—extra stitches must be added rather than simply relying on making each stitch larger.

LIFTED INCREASE

Also referred to as "knit below" or "row below," lifted increases can be slanted to the right or left to make an increase that is barely visible. For that reason, this increase is a good choice for sleeve seams and areas where discreet shaping is required, since it forms a very smooth surface. However, because it draws up the stitch from the previous row, it is best suited to instances where increases are four or more rows apart.

KNIT RIGHT-SLANTING INCREASE

STEP 1
To create an increase that slants to the right, insert the tip of the right needle from front to back going under the right (back) leg of the stitch below the stitch about to be worked.

STEP 2
Knit into this loop, then knit the next stitch as normal.

KNIT LEFT-SLANTING INCREASE

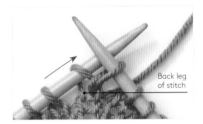

STEP 1
To create an increase that slants to the left, insert the tip of the left needle from back to front into the left (back) leg of the stitch on the row below the stitch that has just been worked.

STEP 2
Take the right needle over the left needle and knit into the back of the loop.

STEP 3
Knit the next stitch as normal.

PURLED RIGHT-SLANTING INCREASE

STEP 1
Holding yarn to the front, insert the left needle from back to front into the stitch below the one just completed on the right needle. Insert the tip of the right needle from back to front into the right (back) leg of the stitch on the left needle.

STEP 2
Keeping the right needle in front of the left and still with the yarn in front, purl and continue as normal.

PURLED LEFT-SLANTING INCREASE

STEP 1
For an increase that slants to the left, with yarn to the front, insert the right needle from left to right into the front of the top of the stitch below the next stitch on the left needle. The right needle goes behind the left needle.

STEP 2
Use the tip of the left needle to go into the front of the stitch just picked up on the right needle. Transfer the stitch onto the left needle.

STEP 3
Purl into this stitch.

RAISED INCREASE (M1)

This increase is also referred to as the strand increase or (particularly in UK patterns) as "make one" (M1). It is made from the strand between two stitches. It can be slanted right or left, which is frequently used as a design feature. For example, a left and right increase may be paired to make the fabric appear to fan out in a V-shape. It is useful because it is formed independently of the neighboring stitches and can therefore be placed exactly where it is needed. However, it can create a small hole, which may not be desirable.

KNIT RIGHT-SLANTING INCREASE

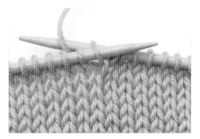

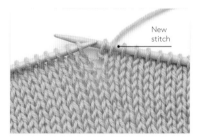

New stitch

STEP 1
For a right-slanting increase on a knit row, insert the tip of the left needle from front to back under the strand of yarn between the stitches on the left and right needles. Hold the loop on the left needle.

STEP 2
Insert the tip of the right needle from front to back into the back of the loop you just put on the left needle. Knit this stitch.

STEP 3
Remove the left needle and note that there is now an extra stitch, formed by knitting into the strand you lifted between the stitches.

KNIT LEFT-SLANTING INCREASE

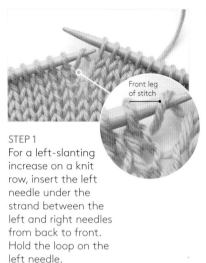

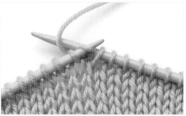

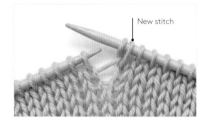

STEP 1
For a left-slanting increase on a knit row, insert the left needle under the strand between the left and right needles from back to front. Hold the loop on the left needle.

STEP 2
Knit into the front of the strand on the left needle.

STEP 3
Still with the yarn to the front, insert the tip of the right needle from the back to the front of the back of the loop on the left needle. Purl this stitch. Remove the left needle and note that there is now an extra stitch, formed by knitting into the strand you lifted between the stitches.

PURLED RIGHT-SLANTING INCREASE

STEP 1
To create a right-slanting increase on a purl row, hold the yarn forward to the front. Use the left needle to pick up the strand between the two needles, inserting the needle from front to back. Hold the loop on the left needle.

STEP 2
Purl into the stitch on the left needle as normal.

STEP 3
Slip the left needle out of the stitch. Note how the new stitch has been made from the strand between the two needles.

PURLED LEFT-SLANTING INCREASE

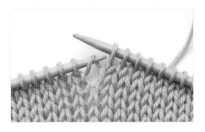  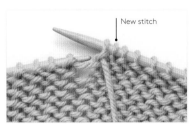

New stitch

STEP 1
For a left-slanting increase on a purl row, hold the yarn at the front. Insert the left needle from back to front under the strand between the left and right needles. Keep the loop on the left needle.

STEP 2
With the right needle in front of the left, insert the right tip up into the front of the loop on the left needle and purl this stitch.

STEP 3
Remove the left needle and note that there is now an extra stitch, formed by knitting into the strand you lifted between the stitches.

YARN OVER INCREASE (YO, YFWD, YF, YRN, WYIF, YON)

There are several variations on this stitch; examples include yarn over (yo), yarn forward (yfwd, yf), yarn around needle (yrn), with yarn in front (wyif), and yarn over/on needle (yon). With these stitches the yarn is simply wrapped around the needle and not worked. The effect of this increase is normally to create a decorative hole in lace patterns.

Yarn over with small hole where new stitch is formed. This will make the eyelet in a lace pattern.

ON A KNIT ROW

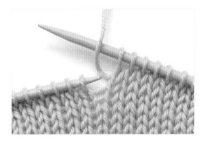  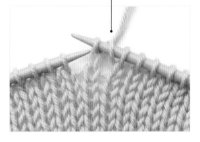

STEP 1
Bring the yarn forward from back to front between the needles, then around the right needle to the back, ready to knit the next stitch. This creates the additional stitch.

STEP 2
Knit the next stitch as normal.

STEP 3
The extra stitch can be seen as a loop just before the knit stitch. The (intentional) hole it creates will be clearly visible after a couple of rows.

ON A PURL ROW OR BEFORE A PURL STITCH

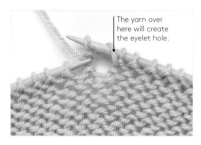

The yarn over here will create the eyelet hole.

STEP 1
Keep the yarn forward as for a normal purl stitch. Take the working yarn around the right needle, going from left to right over the top of the right needle, under the right needle, between the needles, and back to the front.

STEP 2
Being careful to keep the loop around the right needle in place, purl the next stitch as normal.

STEP 3
As with the knit yarn over, a purled yarn over sits before the stitch just purled as a loop rather than a complete stitch.

MULTIPLE INCREASES AND DECREASES

Increasing several stitches at once is normally achieved by casting on stitches. Use a two-needle cast on for this (see page 25). For a stretchier cast on (useful for buttonholes), an alternate cable cast on (see note below) is a good choice.

CABLE CAST ON

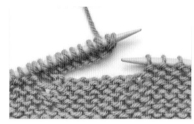

STEP 1
With the worked knitting in your left hand, insert the right needle from front to back between the first two stitches on the left needle.

STEP 2
Make a knit stitch, then return the stitch to the left needle.

STEP 3
When the number of new stitches needed has been made, work the whole row to the end as normal, including the newly made stitches (these will be worked first).

ALTERNATIVE CABLE CAST ON

Purl stitches can be cast on in the same way as the standard two-needle cast on, but alternating between a knit and purl cast on.

For a purl cast on, simply insert the needle between the two stitches from behind, purl as normal, then return the new stitch to the left needle.

Decreasing

Decreases are used to make your knit fabric smaller, as well as to shape necklines and armholes, and for pockets, buttonholes, and other design features.

Interesting effects can be achieved with strategic shaping. For example, a blanket square that is made by increasing from one corner to the center, then decreasing back down to the opposite corner will form a square with a surprisingly different look without affecting the finished shape.

Depending on the type of decrease used, some are barely noticeable and others are intentionally bold for decorative effect. A decrease will normally slant either to the right or left.

DECREASING ON A KNIT ROW

KNIT TWO TOGETHER RIGHT-SLANTING DECREASE (K2TOG)

 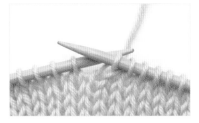

STEP 1
Insert the right needle from front to back into the next two stitches on the left needle.

STEP 2
Wrap the yarn as for a normal knit stitch and knit the two stitches as one.

SLIP, SLIP, KNIT LEFT-SLANTING DECREASE (SSK)

Often paired with a k2tog is the slip, slip, knit (ssk). It gives a neat, left-slanting stitch.

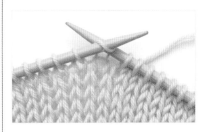 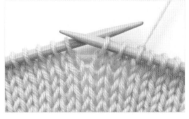

STEP 1
Insert the right needle into the next stitch as if to knit (knitwise).

STEP 2
Slip the stitch onto the right needle without knitting it. Repeat with the next stitch on the left needle. You should have two slipped stitches on the right needle. Note that the stitches should be slipped one at a time.

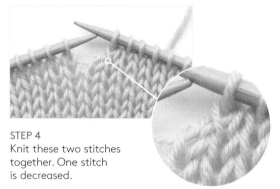

STEP 3
Insert the tip of the left needle from right to left up into the front of the two slipped stitches (the right needle is behind the left needle).

STEP 4
Knit these two stitches together. One stitch is decreased.

SLIP ONE, KNIT ONE, PASS THE SLIPPED STITCH OVER LEFT-SLANTING DECREASE (SL1, K1, PSSO)

This is a popular decrease, frequently worked together with a yarn over in lace knitting.

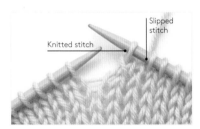

Knitted stitch

Slipped stitch

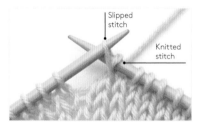

Slipped stitch

Knitted stitch

STEP 1
Insert the right needle as if to knit (knitwise) into the next stitch on the left needle. Slip the stitch onto the right needle without knitting it. Knit the next stitch.

STEP 2
Use the tip of the left needle to lift the slipped stitch over the knit stitch just worked and drop the slipped stitch off the right needle.

CLINIC

MY KNITTING IS VERY TIGHT AND I'M FINDING IT HARD TO MAKE DECREASES. WHAT SHOULD I DO?

When you are starting to knit, it is normal to knit tightly since you are concentrating quite hard and may be worried about dropping stitches.
    If your knitting is very tight, try the following:
- Use a blunt yarn needle to carefully lift one stitch over another when passing slipped stitches over.
- You can also use a yarn needle (or even your fingers) to gently tease out and loosen the stitches, just enough to allow you to insert the needle for knitting stitches together.
- Some beginners find needles with sharper points are helpful, but if you use these, beware of splitting the yarn when knitting.

DECREASING ON A PURL ROW

PURL TWO TOGETHER LEFT-SLANTING DECREASE (P2TOG)

  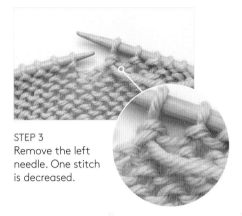

STEP 1
With the yarn forward, insert the tip of the right needle into the front of the first two stitches on the left needle, taking the needle from right to left. The right needle is in front of the left needle.

STEP 2
Wrap the yarn as for a normal purl stitch and purl the two stitches as one.

STEP 3
Remove the left needle. One stitch is decreased.

SLIP, SLIP, PURL (SSP OR SL 2, P SL STS TOG)

STEP 1
Purl until you reach the place where the decrease is to be made. Slip the next two stitches, one at a time, knitwise (as if you were going to knit them), onto the right needle.

STEP 2
Return both stitches one at a time to the left needle.

STEP 3
Insert the right needle from back to front into the back loops of the two slipped stitches on the left needle and purl the two stitches as one.

SLIP ONE, PURL ONE, PASS THE SLIPPED STITCH OVER LEFT-SLANTING DECREASE (SL1, P1, PSSO)

 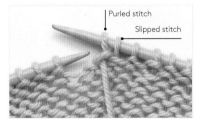 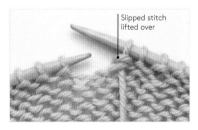

STEP 1
Slip the next stitch knitwise (not purlwise) onto the right needle.

STEP 2
Purl the next stitch.

STEP 3
Lift the slipped stitch over the purled stitch and drop off the right needle.

Binding off

Binding or casting off is essentially a way of removing blocks of stitches in one go. It can be used to finish a piece of work by removing all of the stitches on the needle at once. It can also be used to remove a number of stitches in one go to achieve certain shaping effects.

STANDARD (CHAIN) BIND OFF

This is a popular bind off and creates a firm edge without much elasticity. It is neat and forms a chain of stitches across the top of the work. It can be worked on both a knit or purl row.

STEP 1
Knit (purl) two stitches as normal. Use the tip of the left needle to lift the first stitch knit (purled) on the right needle.

STEP 2
Take this first stitch over the top of the second stitch and drop it off the right needle. One stitch is bound off.

STEP 3
Knit (purl) the next stitch. The second stitch you knit (purled) is then lifted over this stitch and dropped, leaving only the third stitch on the needle. Two stitches are bound off.

STEP 4
Repeat this process until all (or the specified number) of stitches have been bound off.

STEP 5
When you have only one stitch remaining, cut off the working yarn, leaving a tail of around 6in. (15cm). Pass the tail through the stitch and carefully draw up the yarn tight to fasten off. Leave the tail yarn in place for seaming later.

CLINIC

MY CAST OFF IS SO TIGHT MY NEW SOCKS WON'T FIT. WHAT DID I DO WRONG?

It's important to match the bind off to the project. If you need something more stretchy than the standard bind off (for cuffs, necklines, or cowls, for example) look for a stretchy bind off. The example opposite is for a ribbed bind off, but you can follow the same process for a knit bind off. Simply work all the stitches as for the knit stitches (steps 1–3 opposite) and that should add the extra elasticity you need.

JENY'S SUPER-STRETCHY BIND OFF

This straightforward bind off made popular by Jeny Staiman, which she calls her super-stretchy bind off, is a great choice when elasticity is needed, for example with sock cuffs. To work a super-stretchy bind off on a K1, P1 ribbed cuff, follow the instructions below.

STEP 1
As the first stitch is a knit stitch, make a "reverse yarn over" by taking the working yarn from the left needle, under the right needle, from right to left over the top of the needle. (The yarn goes in the opposite direction to normal.)

STEP 2
With the yarn held to the right, knit the next stitch as normal. You will have two stitches on the right needle—the reverse yarn over and the stitch just knit.

STEP 3
On the first stitch only, lift the first stitch (the reverse yarn over) over the stitch just knit.

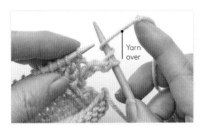

STEP 4
Before the next (purl) stitch, make a yarn over as normal by taking the yarn counterclockwise around the right needle and bringing the yarn around the right needle to the front of the work.

STEP 5
Purl the next stitch as normal. You now have three stitches on the right needle, the stitch left from step 3, the yarn over, and the stitch you just purled.

STEP 6
Using the tip of the left needle, lift the stitch from step 3 and the reverse yarn over from step 4 over the stitch you just purled. You should have one stitch left on the right needle.

STEP 7
On the subsequent knit stitches, make a reverse yarn over by taking the yarn from right to left, over the front of the right needle, between the needles, under the right needle, and holding to the right.

STEP 8
Knit the next stitch. You will have three stitches on the right needle, the stitch from step 6, the reverse yarn over, and the stitch just worked. Using the tip of the left needle, lift the two stitches over the stitch just knit. One stitch remains.

How the finished bind off looks.

Gauge

Mention gauge swatches to most knitters and expect groans! But much as they prevent you from starting that exciting knitting project, they really do save time and disappointment in the long run, so do persevere.

Gauge is simply the size (length x width) of a knitting stitch knit on a specific size of needle using a specified technique. Stitches form the basis of a knit fabric. If you knit your stitches loosely or very tightly, each stitch may be larger or smaller than the ones knit by the designer. This means that even if you are using the same number of stitches as the designer, you may not produce a piece of knitting that is the same size as the one the designer knit.

Small differences over a small square may not seem significant, but if your stitches are just an eighth bigger than the designer's, for every 100 stitches the designer casts on, your work will measure the equivalent of 12 stitches larger. On a shawl with 400 stitches, that's the equivalent of an extra 50 stitches without you having cast on a single extra stitch. Equally, if your square is smaller than the designer's, your garment will be correspondingly smaller—and the greater the difference, the smaller the garment will be.

So, on balance, as frustrating as it may be, making a gauge swatch really is a very worthwhile exercise.

MEASURING GAUGE

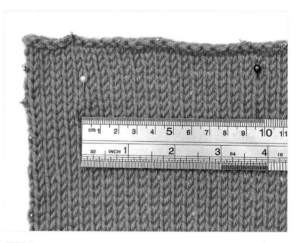

STEP 1
Knit your swatch exactly according to the pattern, bearing in mind that you may be asked to work in a pattern stitch or in a simple stockinette stitch. Knit the swatch 10 or so stitches larger and work an extra 10 rows more than the stated gauge. This allows you to measure in the center of the swatch, which is more accurate since edge stitches are rarely the same size as the main body of the garment and cast-on and bind-off edges can distort your calculations.

STEP 2
Bind off, block, and finish your swatch. Ideally leave it overnight to allow the stitches to settle. Measuring in the center of the swatch, place a pin horizontally straight up one row with a large-headed pin. Use a ruler to measure the stated width (usually 4in./10cm). Measure across the center of the swatch to avoid distortions. Mark this measurement with a second pin. Count the stitches between the two pins. Include any half, quarter, or partial stitches.

CLINIC

HELP! NO MATTER WHICH SIZE NEEDLES I USE, I CAN'T GET THE MEASUREMENTS TO WORK!

Sometimes your knitting will simply not match both the number of rows and the number of stitches simultaneously. Your rows may be correct, but you have too few stitches. When you use larger needles, the stitch numbers are correct, but there are too few rows.

This is quite common and it's worth remembering that your gauge is not inherently "wrong." It's simply that you are matching your knitting to the designer's knitting and you may not knit in quite the same way.

So, what is the answer?

If, having tried a couple of needle sizes, you find that you can't match

both stitches and rows, it is generally advisable to ensure that the number of stitches is correct, even if the number of rows is then different to the pattern.

Where the number of rows is different to the stated gauge, you may need to work fewer/more rows to achieve the correct dimensions. If the pattern gives measurements (e.g. knit until the work measures Xin.), then the number of rows isn't normally important, although you may not end in the same place on the pattern repeat.

Where the pattern requires a specific number of rows, calculate

how many inches this will be based on the stated gauge. Compare this to the length if you used your own gauge and aim to work more/fewer rows to match the original length. If it is a close measurement over a small length, this may not be necessary, but over a long distance, adjustments will be needed.

Aim to adjust length in areas where there is no shaping if at all possible. If you are adjusting rows in an area where stitches will be picked up, you may need to adjust the number of stitches being picked up accordingly.

STEP 3

Starting several rows into the swatch and in the center of the width, place a pin horizontally straight along a line of stitches. Measure the stated length in a straight, vertical line and mark this point with a second pin. Count the rows between the two pins, including any partial rows. If your finished measurements match the pattern, you can proceed knitting with the needles you have been using. If the square is too small, repeat the process using a size larger needles. If the square is too large, try again with smaller needles.

TOP TIPS FOR SUCCESS

- Keep swatches for future reference in a folder or box (carefully labeled!), since these may come in handy if you knit the project or use the same yarn again.

- Swatches can be made into small projects such as coasters, mats, or small purses. They can also be sewn together to create a blanket—a wonderful history of your knitting projects!

- If a pattern is to be knit in the round, make sure to knit your gauge swatch in the round, as gauge is often different when comparing circular to flat knitting.

- Use the same needles as for your correct swatch and remember to adjust any smaller or larger needles (e.g. for ribs or bands) correspondingly.

Essential techniques knitting

BE INSPIRED

1. TUNIC DRESS

Knitting isn't just for sweaters and scarves, as this elegant tunic dress by Emma Middleton shows. A careful combination of texture stitches and simple stockinette stitch with stylish shaping make this a great addition to the wardrobe.

2. BABETTE CARDIGAN

Double seed stitch is simple to work, and gives a richly textured fabric. Combined with the shaped hem, this garment by Sarah Hatton would be a lovely project for an intermediate knitter keen to move on from basic shapes and techniques.

3

4

5

3. COWL
Choosing simple stitches doesn't mean sacrificing style, as this striking cowl by Jen Geigley shows. The use of a bold, chunky yarn with a simple circular technique means you'll only need the absolute basics, but you'll still look great when the weather turns wintery.

4. STRIPED BLANKET
The clever use of color in this luxurious yarn illustrates how the simplest of stitches and shapes can be turned into a look that will stand the test of time. This blanket by Quail Studio is a design that will be in high demand with any parent to be!

5. CABLED BLANKET
The use of bold cable panels in this snuggly blanket by Linda Whaley makes it sumptuously springy and cuddly. Although there is a lot of detail in this design, the cables do repeat, so with careful attention to the pattern, this could be a good project for an intermediate knitter.

Quick start project

Raspberry tote

This is a deceptively easy, quirky tote that is made from a series of simple garter-stitch squares. Joined together with loops of i-cord, this tote opens nice and wide with a flat base, making it an ideal project bag. When you're done, just pull up the cord strap and away you go!

FINISHED SIZE
One size
Each square measures
4³/₄ x 4³/₄in. (12 x 12cm)
Each triangle (excluding the i-cord) measures 4³/₄ x 2¹/₂in. (12 x 6cm)
Total size when flat approximately:
24 x 24in. (60 x 60cm)

GAUGE
22 sts and 50 rows = 4in. (10cm) square using size 5 (3.75mm) needles over garter stitch

YOU WILL NEED
• 5 x 4oz (100g) balls of DK weight yarn; Debbie knitted with Cascade 220 100% superwash wool DK, with approximately 220yd (200m) per ball, in the following five shades (although any DK yarn can be substituted):
  o Color A—Pink Rose (835)
  o Color B—Rose Petal (838)
  o Color C—Pink Ice (836)
  o Color D—Tahitian Rose (914A)
  o Color E—Strawberry Cream (894)
• Pair of size 5 (3.75mm) knitting needles
• 2 x size 3 (3.25mm) double-pointed needles (for i-cord)
• Yarn needle (for sewing up)

ABBREVIATIONS AND TECHNIQUES
DPN(s): double-pointed needle(s)
k: knit (see page 28)
k2tog: knit the next two sts together (see page 41)
kfb: make one by knitting into the front and back of the stitch (one stitch increased) (see page 34)
LH: left hand
rep: repeat
RH: right hand
sl1k2togpsso: slip the next stitch as if to knit, knit the next two stitches together as one stitch, pass the slipped stitch over the stitches just knit together (2 stitches decreased)
st(s): stitch(es)
WS: wrong side
Oversewing (see page 138)

PATTERN NOTES
• The instructions are for one size but can be made larger by adding extra squares and triangles.
• If you choose to make a larger tote, you may need to purchase additional yarn.

MAIN BODY PIECES
Using color A, make 6 squares.
Cast on 2 sts using size 5 (3.75mm) needles.
Row 1: Knit.
Row 2: K1, kfb, k to end.
Rep row 2 until you have 40 sts.
Row 40: Knit.
Row 41: K1, k2tog, k to end.
Rep row 41 until you have 2 sts left.
Row 80: K2tog. (1 st)
Fasten off by cutting off working yarn, leaving a tail of around 12in. (30cm) for sewing up later. Pass the working yarn through the final stitch and draw up tight.

Using color B, make 6 squares following the same pattern as for color A.

Using colors C and E, make 4 two-color squares.
Cast on 2 sts using color C and size 5 (3.75mm) needles.
Row 1: Knit.
Row 2: K1, kfb, k to end.
Rep row 2 until you have 40 sts.
Change to color E and continue in color E as follows:
Row 40: Knit.
Row 41: K1, k2tog, k to end.
Rep row 41 until you have 2 sts left.
Row 80: K2tog. (1 st)
Fasten off by cutting off working yarn, leaving a tail of around 12in. (30cm) for sewing up later. Pass the working yarn through the final stitch and draw up tight.

EDGING TRIANGLES
Using color D, make 16 triangles.
Cast on 28 sts using size 5 (3.75mm) needles.
Row 1: Knit.
Row 2: K1, k2tog, k to end.
Rep row 2 until you have 6 sts left.
Change to size 3 (3.25mm) DPNs and complete the triangle using i-cord as follows:
*Row 24 onward:
1. Knit all the stitches on the needle onto a DPN. Do not turn work, but swap the DPN into the LH and slide the stitches to the other end of the DPN.

DESIGNER'S TIP

The cast-on edge is likely to be a little open. This can be used to your advantage when joining the two ends. Weave in the tail of the bind-off end, then push it a little way inside the cast-on end. Use the other tail to stitch around the join and the ends should be barely visible.

Important: Note that the working yarn is at the left edge of the knitting (this is correct, so don't panic!).

2. Using a second DPN, pull the working yarn tight and knit the stitches off the DPN in the LH onto the new DPN as normal.
3. Swap the DPNs over, slide the stitches on the left needle to the front, pull the working yarn tight, and knit these stitches off onto the RH DPN.

Note: As you knit, pulling the working yarn tight at the start of the row will form the knitting into a tube. It is important to pull tightly to avoid a ladder.

**Binding off: When the cord measures 6in. (15cm), bind off as follows:
Row 1: K1, sl1k2togpsso, k2tog. (3 sts)
Row 2: Sl1k2togpsso. (1 st)
Fasten off by cutting off working yarn, leaving a tail of around 12in. (30cm) for sewing up later. Pass the working yarn through the final stitch and draw up tight.

I-CORD SHOULDER STRAP
Using color E, cast on 6 sts onto a size 3 (3.25mm) DPN. Knit a length of i-cord following the steps from * opposite, until the cord measures 30in. (76cm) or the desired length. Bind off by working from ** above. Fasten off.

MAKING UP THE BAG
Bag body:
1. Lay out the squares in your chosen pattern. I put the two-color squares in the center and alternated the other two colors around the edges.
2. Join the individual squares neatly to form a larger, 4 x 4 square using oversewing.

To attach the triangles:
3. Making sure that the open side of the i-cord is facing toward you, oversew the long (cast-on) edge of each triangle to one outer square. You may need to stretch the triangle a little bit to form the slightly bulbous "raspberry" shape.
4. Repeat for each triangle, making sure that for each triangle the open side of the i-cord faces toward you (i.e. the open ends all point in the same direction, as this will be the WS of the bag).

Join i-cord loops:
1. Fold each i-cord loop so that the end meets the open side. Carefully stitch the end to the open side (on the WS of the bag), making sure that the i-cord isn't twisted.

2. Fasten off each loop and weave in any ends neatly. Thread the long strap through each loop in order. Lift to ensure all loops are threaded and that they are not twisted or crossed over. Neatly stitch the two ends of the i-cord into a long loop. Weave in any ends neatly.

Guest Designer Amanda Kaffka

I learned to knit from my mother when I was six on a pair of knitting needles she whittled out of *Arbutus* twigs. My earliest fiber-craft memories are of going into yarn stores and picking out colors and textures, which led to my obsession with yarn and my extensive stash. A passionate knitwear designer with a degree in fashion design, I base my designs on rhythmical stitches and simple shapes, with a flattering fit. I find inspiration from the city I live in and the places that I visit. I look to nature and urban surroundings, along with movies and TV series, to spark ideas, and am inspired by both trends and timeless classics. I love to sit in a coffee shop with my knitting and a friend while people-watching and sipping a cappuccino. You can follow my adventures on Instagram @amandakaffka and www.thecraftyjackalope.com.

Simple Scarf

Sinking into the rhythm of the fisherman's rib stitch, creating this simple scarf never felt so Zen. Mirroring the look of brioche stitch without the complexity, fisherman's rib is a modified rib that creates a reversible, super-squishy, cozy fabric with great stitch definition.

FINISHED SIZE
9½ x 64in. (24 x 162.5cm) before blocking (excluding the pompoms)

GAUGE
15 sts and 24 rows = 4in. (10cm) square, slightly stretched, using size 10.5 (6.5mm) needles over fisherman's rib

YOU WILL NEED
- MC: 6 x 2oz (50g) balls of 5-ply WoolAddicts EARTH, with approximately 71yd (65m) per ball, in Gold (011)
- CC: 2 x 2oz (50g) balls of 5-ply WoolAddicts EARTH with approximately 71yd (65m) per ball, in Gray (003)
- Pair of size 10.5 (6.5mm) knitting needles
- Large pompom maker
- Removable stitch marker— optional (see Tip)

ABBREVIATIONS AND TECHNIQUES
CC: contrast color
k: knit (see page 28)
MC: main color
p: purl (see page 30)
patt: pattern
rep = repeat
RS: right side
sl1 (RS): slip one stitch purlwise wyif, bring yb between needles to work the next stitch
sl1 (WS): slip one stitch knitwise wyib, bring yf between needles to work the next stitch
st(s): stitch(es)
WS: wrong side
wyib: with yarn in back
wyif: with yarn in front
yb: yarn back
yf: yarn forward
Blocking (see page 141)
Weaving in (see pages 139–140)

MAIN SCARF
Cast on 33 sts using MC and size 10.5 (6.5mm) needles. Work in fisherman's rib patt as follows:
Row 1 (RS): Sl1, *(k1, p1); rep from * to end.
Row 2: Sl1, p1, *(k1 into st below, p1); rep from * to last st, k1.
Row 3: Sl1, *(k1 into st below, p1); rep from * to end.
Rep rows 2 and 3 until piece measures 64in. (162.5cm). Bind off (k1, p1)-wise.

POMPOMS (ALIKE)
Make four pompoms using CC and the large pompom maker. Leave a 15in. (38cm) tail. Using the tail, sew a pompom onto each point of the scarf, two at each end.

TO FINISH
Block knitting to size, omitting the pompoms. Weave in any ends.

DESIGNER'S TIP

Because the fisherman's rib is reversible, distinguishing the RS and WS can be difficult. Place a removable stitch marker on the RS as a reference to help differentiate between rows 2 and 3 while knitting.

3

STITCH PATTERNS
FOR TEXTURE

Once you have mastered the essentials in Chapter 2, you will very quickly be able to combine the stitches you have already learned with some new techniques to create a whole wealth of new projects. In this chapter, we'll be looking at working from charted patterns, why designers use them, and how they work. We'll explore lace and cable stitches and see how we can use them to create texture and interest.

Charted designs

Charts are used to describe knitting patterns in a graphical form. They may be used for an entire project, but normally just illustrate the more complex parts of a design alongside the written information. Charts are particularly useful for lace, cable, and colorwork designs as they make it possible to see the pattern structure more easily and they give a more visual representation of the design.

READING CHARTS—FLAT KNITTING

For projects that are knit flat (as opposed to in the round) the rows on the chart are normally worked starting at the bottom-right corner, reading from right to left for the first row. The next row is then read starting at the left and reading from left to right. For some patterns this may be reversed where, for example, the first row is a wrong side (WS) row. The pattern information and glossary will tell you if this is the case.

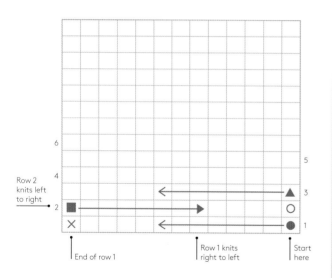

At the end of row 1, X is the final stitch knitted. Because the work is turned when knitting flat, row 2 begins at the square symbol and ends at the circle symbol. Row 3, after turning the work, begins at the triangle symbol.

READING CHARTS— KNITTING IN THE ROUND

When reading charts that are written for knitting in the round (also called circular knitting), each line in the chart is read in the same direction, usually starting at the bottom-right corner and reading from right to left.

This is because when you knit in the round you are always knitting in the same direction, usually from right to left and the work never swaps hands. When you make a flat piece of knitting, the work is knit from the right edge to the left, swapped back into the left hand, and knit from the left edge to the right.

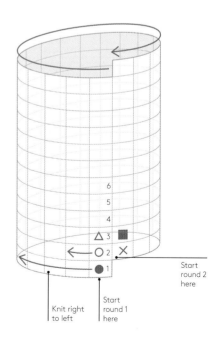

At the end of the round of knitting, X is the final stitch of round 1. The next stitch to be knitted is the first stitch of round 2. When knitting in the round, this is the circle symbol. The final stitch of round 2 is the square symbol. The first stitch of round 3 is the triangle symbol.

UNDERSTANDING CHARTS AND HOW TO USE THEM

SYMBOLS, STITCH KEY, AND ABBREVIATIONS/GLOSSARY

On a chart, each stitch (or combination of stitches) will be allocated a symbol. The symbols will be listed alongside either an abbreviation or explanation of the stitch in a key. If it shows an abbreviation, the full explanation can be found in the stitch "glossary."

As not all patterns use the same symbols, it is crucial to read and refer to the key. Unlike written patterns, charts may use the same symbol for two stitches—usually one to represent a stitch when worked on the RS and one for the WS. For example, in the chart below, the solid circle represents a purl stitch when worked on a RS row. On a WS row, however, it represents a knit stitch. This small chart would create a border of garter stitch at each edge with a section of stockinette stitch in the middle, as follows:

Cast on 7 sts.
Row 1 (RS): Knit
Row 2 (WS): P2, k3, p2. 7 sts.
Repeat rows 1–2.

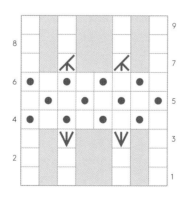

RS: knit
WS: purl

RS: purl
WS: knit

3-stitch
repeat

NO STITCH

Where a stitch is decreased on a chart (and so does not exist for the remainder of the section), a gray square is often used to depict that there is no longer a stitch to be worked. This may be described as "no stitch" in the abbreviations. In this example, the equivalent written pattern would read as follows:

Cast on 4 sts.
Row 1 (RS): Knit. 4 sts.
Row 2 (WS): Purl.
Row 3: K1, (kfbf) twice, k1. 8 sts.
Row 4: *k1, p1; rep from * to end.
Row 5: *p1, k1; rep from * to end.
Row 6: Repeat row 4.
Row 7: K1, (k3tog) twice, k1. 4 sts.
Row 8: Purl.
Row 9: Knit.
Note how the stitch numbers increase on row 4 and decrease on row 8 and that the chart is read straight across, effectively ignoring the gray squares.

knit

RS: purl
WS: knit

RS: knit into fbf
WS: purl into fbf

no stitch

RS: k3tog
WS: p3tog

SQUARES AND SPANS

Each stitch of knitting is represented by one square on the chart. Where a stitch is worked using several stitches, for example lace, cables, and some special patterns, these stitches will extend over a number of squares. This denotes that these stitches are worked as a unit.

Cast on 10 sts.
Row 1 (RS): P3, k4, p3. 10 sts.
Row 2 and all WS rows: K3, p4, k3.
Row 3: Repeat row 1.
Row 5: P3, 2/2 LC, p3.
Rows 7 and 9: Repeat row 1.
Row 11: Repeat row 5.

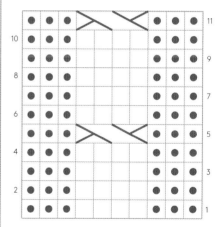

RS: knit
WS: purl

RS: purl
WS: knit

2/2 LC

ROW NUMBERING

Where alternate rows are identical, to save printing space the chart may only show every other row. This will be clear from the row numbering (usually printed vertically up the side of the chart), where only every other row will be numbered. Alternately, the key may have instructions to treat every alternate row as, for example, a purl row.

The two charts below cover the same number of rows and produce the same pattern, but chart A shows every row, whereas chart B shows just alternate rows:

Rows 1–6: *k1, p1; rep from * to end.

PATTERN REPEATS

Where a pattern is repeated several times across a row, the chart will normally show the pattern section just once (this is referred to as the "pattern repeat"). To allow for different sizes and for shaping, there may be some stitches at the beginning or end of the row that are only worked once. The pattern repeat is usually surrounded by a bold or colored line. This row, for example, would read:

Cast on a multiple of 2 sts plus 6
Row 1 (RS): P3, k to last 2 sts, p3.
Row 2 and all WS rows: K3, p to last 2 sts, k3.
Row 3: Repeat row 1.
Row 5: P3, *yo, k2tog; rep from * to last 2 sts, p3.
Repeat rows 2–5.

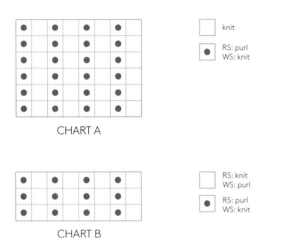

CHART A

	knit
●	RS: purl WS: knit

CHART B

	RS: knit WS: purl
●	RS: purl WS: knit

For the PATTERN REPEATS chart key:

	RS: knit WS: purl
●	RS: purl WS: knit
O	yo
/	RS: k2tog WS: p2tog
	2-stitch repeat
	Set-up row repeat

In this example, the first three stitches and the final three stitches are only worked once. In the chart, we can see this as they sit outside the red lines. If we wanted a bigger piece of knitting, we could cast on—for example, 36 (30+6) sts, 146 (140+6) sts, or even 4006 (4000+6) sts. As long as the multiple is correct we use that number and add the extra stitches just once.

Note also that the first row sits outside the red lines but is within a blue box. This means that the first row is only worked once, but the section outlined in blue is repeated to the end of that row. This may be referred to in patterns as a "set-up" row as it sets up the pattern.

SIZING

Where a chart needs to show multiple sizes you may see additional boxed-out sections to show the instructions for different sizes. Be careful to follow the correct section for your size. For example, if you were making the second size, you would work as follows:

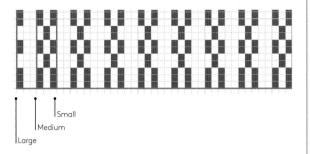

Small
Medium
Large

COLOR CHARTS

Fair Isle and colorwork often use colored charts. Each colored square represents a different color yarn. Be sure to make a note of which color on the chart represents the color you are knitting with.

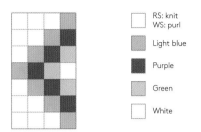

☐ RS: knit
WS: purl

▨ Light blue

▧ Purple

▨ Green

☐ White

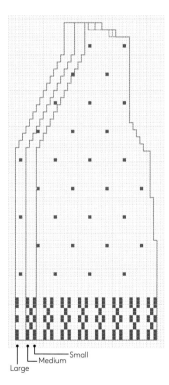

Small
Medium
Large

💡 **TOP TIPS FOR WORKING WITH CHARTS**
•••••••••••••••••••••••••••••••••••••

- Photocopy (and enlarge if necessary) your charts and use a piece of masking tape to show which row you are on.

- Mark off rows as you complete them with a highlighter pen. If you need to reuse the chart, use a different pen or cross through the highlighter.

- Don't be tempted to cross out completed lines—just in case you make a mistake!

- Mark out your size with a highlighter pen if appropriate.

- Photocopy the key and keep it next to you for easy reference.

- Copy the color chart and attach a small piece of the relevant color yarn next to each color on the chart for easy reference.

- Use "lifelines" for complicated projects such as lace (see page 60).

- A cable or lace panel, perhaps down a plain sleeve or along the edges of a knitted throw, can add a stylish touch to an otherwise simple knit. Remember that cables and lace pattern stitches can affect the drape, density, and feel of the knitted fabric, so careful swatching is essential.

MULTIPLE CHARTS

To save space, where there are several areas of pattern in a piece, there may be a number of small charts. You will be instructed which chart to follow at the appropriate part in the text.

Introducing lace

To the first-time lace knitter, it can be hard to imagine mastering such apparently difficult patterns. However, most lace stitches are created using straightforward combinations of yarn overs and decreases.

The yarn over creates the hole or eyelet, but at the same time it creates an additional stitch. To maintain even edges and keep the number of stitches constant, a compensating decrease must be worked for each yarn over. It is this combination of increases and decreases that creates the wonderful patterns seen in so many designs, from gossamer-light shawls through to lacy socks, sweaters, accessories, and even jewelry.

UNDERSTANDING LACE TERMINOLOGY

There are some terms that feature in lace patterns and which you may read on forums. They may sound unusual, but once you know what they mean all will become clear.

RESTING ROW
A resting row is one where there is no shaping and there are no lace stitches. Essentially you are having a rest from following the lacy pattern!

LIFELINE
When working lace patterns, many knitters use "lifelines." A lifeline is simply a piece of smooth yarn (e.g. cotton) in a contrasting color that is

threaded through a complete row of stitches at regular intervals, usually at the start of a pattern repeat. This helps limit the number of rows that need unpicking if an error is made.

BLOCKING
When some lace projects come off the needles, they look very crumpled and shapeless. Blocking describes the process of carefully stretching out the project to its intended shape. It is possible to buy specific frames or boards for this process, but the interlocking foam mats that you can buy for children's playrooms are ideal for pinning out and finishing your knits.

YARN OVER (YO, YF, YFWD) KNIT FOLLOWED BY KNIT STITCH

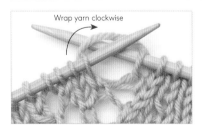

Wrap yarn clockwise

STEP 1
To create an eyelet in a knit row, first make a yarn over (also referred to as a yarn forward). Knit to where the yarn over is to be made. Bring the yarn under the right needle to the front of the work, over the needle, and hold at the back ready to make the next stitch.

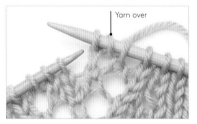

Yarn over

STEP 2
Knit the next stitch as normal.

Yarn over

STEP 3
When a yarn over has been made on a knit row, it will normally be worked (usually purled, but in some patterns, knitted) on the following row. The yarn over can be identified as it looks almost like a loop of loose thread rather than a complete stitch.

YARN AROUND NEEDLE (YRN) KNIT FOLLOWED BY PURL STITCH

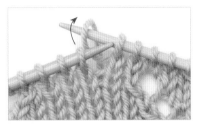

STEP 1
Bring the yarn under the right needle to the front, then take it over the right needle and hold to the back.

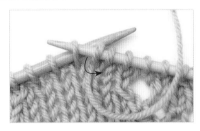

STEP 2
Yarn over now complete. To work the next stitch, bring the yarn under the right needle again to the front and purl.

MULTIPLE YARN OVER—FOR LARGER EYELETS OR LONG STITCHES

STEP 1
Bring the yarn under the right needle to the front of the work, then over the needle. Continue wrapping around the needle for the number of times stated in the pattern.

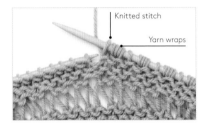

STEP 2
Knit the next stitch, leaving the wraps in place (visible as loops around the right needle).

STEP 3
On the following row, the extra wraps are normally dropped, creating large eyelets.

CENTRAL DOUBLE DECREASE (CDD, S2KP2, S2KP, SL2KP, SL2K1P2SSO)— TWO DECREASES AROUND A CENTRAL STITCH

This stitch is often used to create the central "spine" of a shawl or for shell and wave patterns as it creates a balanced, clearly defined V-shape.

STEP 1
Slip two stitches knitwise (as if to knit) onto the right needle without knitting them.

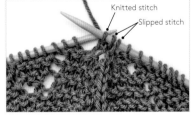

STEP 2
Knit the next stitch.

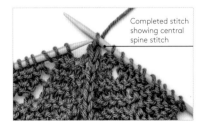

STEP 3
Using the tip of the left needle, lift both slipped stitches over the knit stitch just made, and allow them to drop off the needle.

YARN OVER SLIP ONE KNIT ONE PASS SLIPPED STITCH OVER (YOSKP/YO, SL1, PSSO)— INCREASE AND DECREASE AT THE SAME TIME

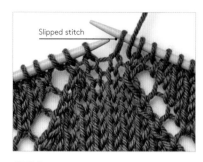

STEP 1
With the yarn held at the front, slip the next stitch from the left hand to the right needle as if to knit, but without actually knitting it.

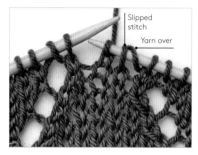

STEP 2
Knit the next stitch, leaving the slipped stitch unworked in between the yarn over and the knitted stitch. As the stitch is knitted, the yarn over can be seen as a loop of thread over the needle rather than as a complete stitch.

STEP 3
With the left needle, lift the slipped stitch over the stitch just knitted, decreasing one stitch. This decrease compensates for the stitch increased when making the yarn over.

STEP 4
Drop the lifted stitch off the right needle. The yarn over can be seen as a loop and will be worked on the next row. This method is usually abbreviated in patterns to "yo, sl1, k1, psso" (yarn over, slip 1, knit 1, pass slipped stitch over).

Level:
Advanced

Yarn:
Lace weight to bulky

Stitches:
Multiple of 10 sts
plus 3

Repeat:
6-row pattern repeat

	RS: knit
	WS: purl

•	RS: purl
	WS: knit

╱	RS: k2tog
	WS: p2tog

O	RS: yo
	WS: yo

╲	RS: ssk
	WS: p2tog tbl

	RS: gray no stitch
	WS: gray no stitch

V	RS: slip purlwise with yarn in front
	WS: slip

	Variable sts repeat (16 sts max)

Vertical ripple lace pattern

The yarn over row in this pattern creates a ripple in the fabric, which is then reduced with decreases in later rows (meaning that not all rows have the same number of stitches). It creates a lovely, richly textured fabric that can be used as an accent feature or an all-over pattern.

Cast on a multiple of 10 sts plus 3.
Row 1 (RS): *K1, sl1 wyif, k1, k2tog, (yo, k1) x 5, yo, ssk; rep from * to last 3 sts, k1, sl1 wyif, k1. 19 sts.
Row 2 (WS): K1, p1, k1, *p13, k1, p1, k1; rep from * to end.
Row 3: *K1, sl1 wyif, k1, k2tog, k9, ssk; rep from * to last 3 sts, k, sl1 wyif, k1. 17 sts.
Row 4: K1, p1, k1, *p11, k1, p1, k1; rep from * to end.
Row 5: *K1, sl1 wyif, k1, k2tog, k7, ssk; rep from * to last 3 sts, k1, sl1 wyif, k1. 15 sts.
Row 6: K1, p1, k1, *p9, k1, p1, k1; rep from * to end.

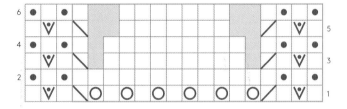

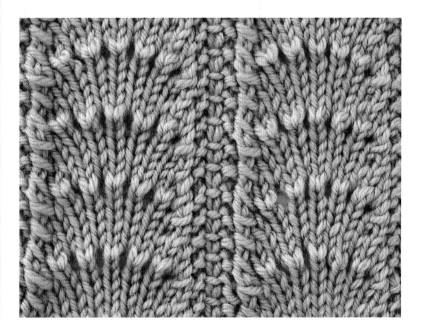

Introducing cables

A familiar feature in Aran sweaters and Ganseys, cables, honeycombs, twisted, and traveling stitches are now widely used in samplers, afghans, and accessories.

Cables are essentially combinations of knit and purl stitches where the stitches are worked out of sequence. A simple cable may comprise a single braid; more intricate combinations are used to produce intertwining plaits, honeycombs, and lattices. To create a simple cable, stitches are transferred to a short needle (a cable needle) and these stitches are then held either at the front or the back of the knitting. A number of stitches are then knitted from the main needle. To complete the sequence, the stitches from the cable needle are then knitted. This has the effect of creating a crossed fabric. Where stitches are held at the back, the cross will be to the right. Stitches held at the front will create a cross moving to the left.

SIMPLE FOUR-STITCH CABLE TWISTING TO THE LEFT

Cables are often set on a background of reverse stockinette stitch. This is where the purl side of stockinette stitch is used as the right side of the work rather than the more usual knit side. This gives the cable more definition, as it stands out more clearly from the background.

STEP 1
Work to where the cable begins. Using the cable needle, lift the first stitch off the left needle as if to purl (purlwise).

STEP 2
Keeping the first stitch on the cable needle, lift the next stitch purlwise from the left needle onto the cable needle.

STEP 3
To create a cable that travels (twists) to the left, the stitches on the cable needle are held in front of the work. Slide the stitches to the middle of the cable needle to prevent them sliding off.

STEP 4
Allow the cable needle to rest at the front of the work. Tuck the left end carefully into the knitting, being careful not to split the yarn if necessary. Knit the next stitch.

STEP 5
Knit the next stitch from the left needle. This may feel awkward and the stitches quite tight. This is normal. The stitches need to be quite tight to avoid an unsightly hole at the edge of the cable.

STEP 6
Pick up or untuck the cable needle from the fabric and slide the stitches on the cable needle to the right hand.

STEP 8
Knit the next stitch from the cable needle. Set the cable needle to one side and return to working the stitches on the left needle. Draw up the first stitch firmly to avoid a hole (see below).

STEP 7
Hold the cable needle in the left hand in front of the left needle. Keeping the cable needle parallel and close to the left needle will reduce stretching. Knit the first stitch from the cable needle.

CLINIC

I'M WORKING WITH A CABLE PATTERN AND THE CHART IS CONFUSING. HOW CAN I MAKE THE PROCESS EASIER?

When working cables, the symbols on charts can seem quite similar. Invest in a set of highlighter pens and mark each cable type with a different color to make the chart easier to follow.

☐	RS: knit WS: purl
▣	RS: purl WS: knit
⧄	RS: 1/1 LC WS: 1/1 LC
⧅	RS: 1/1 RC WS: 1/1 RC
⬚	RS: 2/2 LC WS: 2/2 LC
⬚	RS: 2/2 RC WS: 2/2 RC

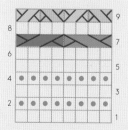

SIMPLE FOUR-STITCH CABLE TWISTING TO THE RIGHT

For a cable that twists to the right, the stitches on the cable needle are held at the back of the work instead of the front.

STEP 1
Work to where the cable begins. Using the cable needle, lift the first stitch off the left needle as if to purl (purlwise).

STEP 2
Keeping the first stitch on the cable needle, lift the next stitch purlwise from the left needle onto the cable needle. Slide the stitches to the middle of the cable needle to prevent them sliding off.

STEP 3
To create a cable that travels (twists) to the right, lift the cable needle over the work and allow it to rest at the back of the work, tucking it carefully into the knitting if it feels like the stitches are slipping off.

STEP 4
Still with the cable at the back, knit the next two stitches from the left needle, drawing the yarn quite tight to prevent holes.

STEP 5
Bring the cable needle to the front, slide the stitches to the right end, and knit the next two stitches one at a time off the cable needle. Be careful not to twist the cable needle when you start knitting the stitches.

STEP 6
When you have knitted the stitches from the cable needle, set it to one side and return to working the stitches on the left needle. Draw up the first stitch firmly to avoid a hole.

CABLES MADE EASY

- If your stitches are dropping off your cable needle, try using a cranked or hook version. Alternatively, a tiny rubber band on each end can help—it's a little fussy, but it does work.

- If you notice gaps or holes at the edges of your cables, this usually means you need to pull the yarn a little tighter when knitting the stitches off the cable needle. You can also try using a slightly smaller cable needle, as this prevents the stitches stretching on the cable needle and allows them to be knitted off more easily.

- A magnetic chart holder is great if you have one to mark your place. Sticky notes placed below the row you're working on are also a great idea because you can also jot notes on them, too.

Level:
Beginner

Yarn:
Lace weight to bulky

Stitches:
Multiple of 4 sts plus 6

Repeat:
5-row repeat

Abbreviations

t2Lp: on RS and WS, p into back of 2nd st, then k into front of 1st st, sl both sts of L needle tog

t2Rp: on RS, k into front of 2nd st, then p into front of st on 1st st, sl both sts off L needle tog. On WS, k into front of 2nd st, then p into back of 1st st, sl both sts off L needle tog

Cluster 2: [sl 2 purlwise, yf, return sts to L needle, yb] 3 times, sl2 purlwise

 RS: knit
WS: purl

 RS: purl
WS: knit

 t2Lp

 t2Rp

 Cluster 2

Mock smocking

This pattern uses wrapped stitches to create a lovely, springy fabric with quite a dense texture. It is particularly effective for warm, cozy blankets, adding bounce without too much weight.

Cast on a multiple of 4 sts plus 6.
Row 1 (RS): K2, *p2, k2; rep from * to end.
Row 2: Cluster 2, *k2, cluster 2; rep from * to end.
Row 3: K1, *t2Lp, t2Rp; rep from * to last st, k1.
Row 4: P1, k1, cluster 2, *k2, cluster 2; rep from * to last 2 sts, k1, p1.
Row 5: K1, *t2Rp, t2Lp; rep from * to last st, k1.

Pattern notes
• When working the cluster, pull firmly on the yarn so the wraps pull the stitches together and lie neatly.
• The first row is not repeated, rows 2–5 form the pattern

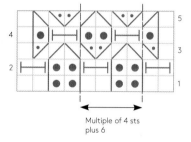

Multiple of 4 sts
plus 6

SIMPLE MOCK CABLES

Mock cables are created by manipulating the stitches with your fingers rather than using a cable needle. This technique does need a little bit of practice to get the tension right, so practice on your swatch until you feel confident.

GET CREATIVE WITH YOUR CABLES

- Adapt a simple cable design and use it as the band for a jacket or to trim a throw or wrap.

- Practice your cables by knitting up your sample squares and stitching them together to create some bold, cozy blankets.

- Combine cables to create more detailed, all-over designs. A simple cable either side of a honeycomb or lattice, for example, looks great.

- Don't have access to knitting software? You can plan your cables using knitters' graph paper. Knitters' graph paper is used because knit stitches aren't usually square, so a chart that has the same proportions as your knitting will give a better idea of the eventual look of the design. You can download free graph paper from the internet.

- Mix in some colorwork (see Chapter 5). Make your cables in different colors for added dramatic effect.

STEP 1
Cast on 10 stitches. P5, take the yarn to the back of the work, and slip the next stitch purlwise to the right needle.

STEP 2
Knit the next eight stitches. Slip the next stitch purlwise to the right needle. Purl to the end of the row.

STEP 3
On the next row, K5, bring the yarn to the front of the work, and slip the next stitch as if to purl (purlwise).

STEP 4
P8, slip the next stitch purlwise, take the yarn to the back of the work, and knit to the end of the row. Repeat steps 1–4.

STEP 5
P5, take the yarn to the back of the work, carefully slide the stitch slipped off the left needle, and let it rest at the front of the work. This slipped stitch will be taken across the next four stitches to create the curve of the cable, moving from right to left, into the center.

STEP 6
Knit the next four stitches. Lift the dropped stitch onto the right needle. Check the lifted stitch is not twisted. If it is, use the left needle (or your fingers!) to return it to the correct shape, as shown above. If the stitch is small, it can be gently drawn out to allow it to reach the left needle without distorting the work.

STEP 7
For the left side of the cable, with the yarn held at the back of the work, slip the next four stitches purlwise to the right needle. Drop the next stitch (the stitch that has been slipped on previous rows) to the front of the work. This dropped stitch will form the left curve of the cable, moving left to right.

STEP 8
Return the four slipped stitches on the right needle to the left needle. Lift the slipped stitch as before and return it to the left needle.

STEP 9
Ensure the stitch is not twisted, then knit this and the next four stitches to form the left curve of the cable, moving left to right. Again, use the needle or fingers to untwist the stitch if needed. Purl to the end of the row.

STEP 10
This completes the cable. The slipped stitches meet in the center, finishing off the mock cable. Note how the slipped stitches should look: smooth, flat, and elongated. For the final row, k5, p10, k5.

CLINIC

I'M FINDING IT HARD TO SEE MY STITCHES. IS THERE ANYTHING I CAN DO?

It's much easier to knit in daylight where possible, especially if you're working with dark yarn. If you are knitting in the evenings, a lamp with a daylight-balanced light bulb will prove really useful. There are also magnifiers on the market that are mainly aimed at embroiderers, but they can be handy for knitters too, particularly when counting and checking stitches.

You can also try placing a piece of dark card (or white if using dark yarn) behind your knitting at regular intervals to help you see the pattern. This makes it easier to see the eyelets and spot errors.

Level:
Beginner

Yarn:
Lace weight to bulky

Stitches:
Multiple of 5 sts
plus 1

Repeat:
6-row pattern repeat

 RS: knit
WS: purl

 RS: purl
WS: knit

 2/2 LC

5-stitch repeat

Four-stitch left-twist cable

Work this easy single cable as a striking panel down a sleeve or front of a garment. By using the left and right twist it can be mirrored to create a balanced panel. Placing additional plain rows between the cable rows will produce a more elongated, soft cable. Reducing the plain rows will give a denser rope effect.

Cast on a multiple of 5 sts plus 1.
Row 1 (RS): *P1, k4; repeat from * to last st, k1. 6 sts.
Row 2 and all WS rows: K1, *p4, k1; repeat from * to end.
Row 3: Repeat row 1.
Row 5: *P1, 2/2 LC; repeat from * to last st, p1.
Repeat rows 1–6.

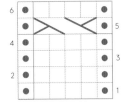

Level:
Advanced

Yarn:
Fingering to worsted

Stitches:
Multiple of 12 sts
plus 2

Repeat:
8-row pattern repeat

	RS: knit WS: purl
	RS: 2/2 RC WS: 2/2 RC
	RS: 2/2 LC WS: 2/2 LC
	RS: purl WS: knit
	RS: 1/1 RC WS: 1/1 RC
	RS: 1/1 LC WS: 1/1 LC
	Multiple of 12 sts plus 2 pattern repeat

Snakes and ladders cable

Two-stitch cable "snakes" surround garter-stitch ladders to create a dense, detailed cable pattern. This pattern requires a little additional attention because there are several different cables being worked at once, but it is quite manageable.

Cast on a multiple of 12 sts plus 2.
Row 1 (RS): Knit. 14 sts.
Row 2 (WS): P2, *p4, k2, p6; repeat from * to end.
Row 3: *1/1 RC, k10; repeat from * to last 2 sts, 1/1 RC.
Row 4: *P6, k2, p4; repeat from * to last 2 sts, p2.
Row 5: K1, *2/2 RC, k4, 2/2 LC; repeat from * to last st, k1.
Row 6: Repeat row 4.
Row 7: *1/1 LC, k10; repeat from * to last 2 sts, 1/1 LC.
Row 8: Repeat row 4.
Row 9: *1/1 RC, k1, 2/2 LC, 2/2 RC, k1; repeat from * to last 2 sts, 1/1 RC.
Row 10: Repeat row 4.
Repeat rows 3–10.

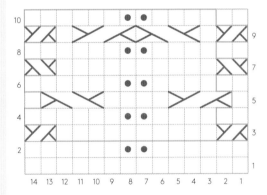

Level:
Beginner

Yarn:
Fingering to bulky

Stitches:
Multiple of 8 sts plus 6

Repeat:
8-row pattern repeat

Abbreviations

3/3 RC: 6-stitch right cable.
Slip 3 sts to cable needle and
hold in back, k3, k3 from
cable needle.

RS: knit
WS: purl

RS: purl
WS: knit

3/3 RC

8-stitch repeat

Six-stitch single cable

Here, shown on a background of reverse stockinette stitch, this simple, mid-width cable is strong enough to be a statement piece, but could also be incorporated with other stitches to create a larger panel. This cable looks great in a wide range of yarns, from fingering to bulky.

6-Stitch Cable Right Twist
Panel: 6 sts

Row 1 (RS): P4, *k6, p2; rep from * to last 2 sts, p2.
Row 2: K2, *k2, p6; repeat from * to last 4 sts, k4.
Row 3 and 4: Repeat Rows 1 and 2.
Row 5: P4, *3/3 RC, p2; repeat from * to last 2 sts, p2.
Row 6: Repeat row 4.
Row 7: Repeat row 1.
Row 8: Repeat row 4.

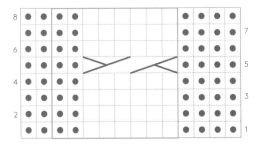

Level:
Beginner

Yarn:
Fingering to bulky

Stitches:
Multiple of 8 sts plus 6

Repeat:
8-row pattern repeat

Abbreviations

3/3 LC: 6-stitch left cable.
Slip 3 sts to cable needle and
hold in front, k3, k3 from
cable needle.
3/3 RC: 6-stitch right cable.
Slip 3 sts to cable needle and
hold in back, k3, k3 from
cable needle.

RS: knit
WS: purl

RS: purl
WS: knit

3/3 RC

8-stitch repeat

3/3 LC

Six-stitch wiggle cable

Two versions of this easy cable pattern are produced by varying the number of plain rows between the cable rows. By working the twist in alternating directions one cable appears to snake over the top of the other, creating a deep texturing.

Short-Length Wiggle Cable
Panel: 6 sts

Row 1 (RS): P4, *k6, p2; repeat from * to last 2 sts, p2.
Row 2: K2, *k2, p6; repeat from * to last 4 sts, k4.
Row 3: P4, *3/3 RC, p2; repeat from * to last 2 sts, p2.
Row 4: Repeat row 2.
Row 5: Repeat row 1.
Row 6: Repeat row 2.
Row 7: P4, *3/3 LC, p2; repeat from * to last 2 sts, p2.
Row 8: Repeat row 4.

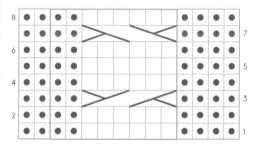

Texture knitting
BE INSPIRED

1. BUBBLY SCARF
Irresistibly snuggly, this bold but straightforward texture pattern by Martin Storey could be readily attempted by a confident beginner. Knitted in a super-bulky yarn, it would be quick to make too!

2. COWLAM SWEATER
Setting this interesting cable by Lisa Richardson against a smooth stockinette-stitch background, rather than the more usual reverse stockinette stitch, gives it a subtler, more gentle effect reminiscent of droplets down a windowpane. The simple set-in sleeve makes the cable pattern easier to work around the upper body shaping.

3. SILVIA SWEATER

A pattern for the more experienced knitter, or an intermediate knitter looking to stretch their skills, this richly textured lattice cable looks great against the garter-stitch background. The design by Sari Nordlund also includes twisted cable stitches in the hem cuff and neckline for added interest.

4. CABLED HEADBAND

Be the talk of the slopes with this richly textured, stylish headband and mitt set by Saara Toikka. Mitts are a great choice for extreme cold, as they are quick to take on and off (handy for the *glüwein* during après-ski time!).

5. HAZE CARDIGAN

Large projects can seem daunting but by using a super-bulky yarn and a simple garter stitch for the main body, this jacket by Quail Studio should knit up in no time. The bold use of giant bobbles adds eye-catching interest.

Quick
start
project

Cabled cowl

This richly textured cowl looks complicated, but there are only
two cable rows. Easing you in with a garter-stitch band, you'll
be moving on to a straightforward cable worked over 10 stitches.
Repeat the two sections until you reach your chosen length,
join the ends together, and no one will know how you did it!

FINISHED SIZE
One size (adjustable to suit)
Width (all sizes): 5³⁄₄in. (14.5cm)

GAUGE
22 sts and 28 rows = 4in. (10cm) square using size
7 (4.5mm) needles over stockinette stitch

YOU WILL NEED
- 1 x 4oz (100g) ball of DK weight yarn; Debbie
  knitted with Cascade 220 100% superwash wool
  DK, with approximately 220yd (200m) per ball,
  using Magenta (908) [although any DK yarn
  can be substituted]
- Pair of size 7 (4.5mm) knitting needles
- Yarn needle (for sewing up)
- Cable needle

ABBREVIATIONS AND TECHNIQUES
5/5 LC: 5/5 (10-stitch) left-twist cable
(see page 64)
5/5 RC: 5/5 (10-stitch) right-twist cable
(see page 66)
k: knit (see page 28)
p: purl (see page 30)
rep: repeat
RS: right side
st(s): stitch(es)
WS: wrong side
Seaming (see pages 136–138)
Weaving in (see pages 139–140)
Blocking (see page 141)

PATTERN NOTES
- The instructions are for one size, but the cowl
  can be lengthened by adding extra repeats.
- Remember that the two ends will be joined
  together, so aim to work a complete pair of
  repeats cable or two garter stitch sections.
- If you choose to lengthen the cowl, you may
  need to purchase additional yarn.

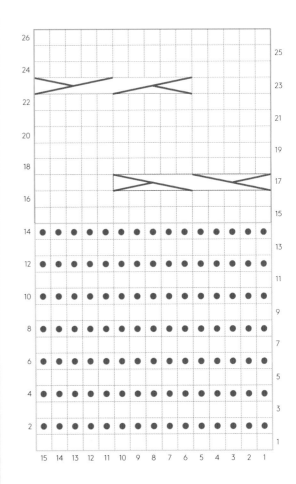

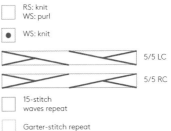

| | RS: knit |
| | WS: purl |

| ● | WS: knit |

| | 5/5 LC |
| | 5/5 RC |

| | 15-stitch |
| | waves repeat |

| | Garter-stitch repeat |

Cast on 45 sts using size 7 (4.5mm) needles
Either follow the written instructions or follow the charted instructions. Both are given below to allow you to compare the two approaches.

WRITTEN INSTRUCTIONS
Rows 1—14: Knit.
Rows 16, 18, 20, 22, 24, and 26 (WS): Purl. (45 sts)
Rows 15, 17, 21, and 23: Knit.
Row 19: *5/5 LC, k5; rep from * to end.
Row 25: *K5, 5/5 RC; rep from * to end.
Rep rows 15–26 twice more (3 chart repeats worked in total).
Rep rows 1–7.
Rep rows 7–18 three times.
Rep rows 1–7.
Rep rows 7–18 three times.
Bind off, not too tightly.

CHART VERSION
To work from the chart, proceed as follows:
*Cast on 45 sts.
Work rows 1–26.
Rep chart rows 1–26 twice.
Rep from * 3 times more (you should have four blocks of garter stitch and four cable blocks in total).
Bind off, not too tightly.

TO FINISH
Block the work and, with WS together, stitch the cast on to the bind-off edge. Weave in any ends.

Guest Designer Diane Ugo

I live in London with my husband and four children. I learned to knit when I was about eight, but then only knitted on and off before stopping completely. I started knitting again when I discovered that I was having triplets. At this point, I also learned how to crochet after seeing a work colleague making a blanket. My first design project was a cowl back in 2011 or 2012. Since then, I've enjoyed designing knitting and crochet patterns, and like to find inspiration in the shapes and patterns around me. My preferred patterns, especially when it comes to designing, are items that look unique but aren't unnecessarily complicated to work up.

Baby's shawl

A fine lace shawl is the perfect gift to welcome a new baby.

FINISHED SIZE
18 x 27in. (46 x 68cm)

GAUGE
When making a gauge swatch, two pattern repeats should measure the following dimensions:
2 patt reps (16 sts) to 3in. (7.5cm)
2 patt reps (24 rows) to 2¾in. (7cm)
See also Designer's Tip, opposite.

YOU WILL NEED
• 1 x 4oz (100g) ball of 3-ply weight yarn; Diane knitted with Stylecraft Wondersoft 3-ply, with approximately 619yd (566m) per ball, using Vanilla [although any 3-ply yarn can be used]
• Pair of size 6 (4mm) knitting needles
• Pair of size 3 (3.25mm) knitting needles
• Yarn needle

ABBREVIATIONS AND TECHNIQUES
k: knit (see page 28)
k2tog: knit the next two sts together (see page 41)
p: purl (see page 30)
patt: pattern
rep: repeat
RS: right side
skpo: slip the next stitch, knit the next stitch, pass the slipped stitch over the knitted stitch
sl1k2togpsso: slip the next stitch as if to knit, knit the next two stitches together as one stitch, pass the slipped stitch over the stitches just knit together (2 stitches decreased)
st(s): stitch(es)
yo: yarn over (see page 60)
Ytrn: yarn twice around needle
WS: wrong side
Oversewing (see page 138)
Blocking (see pages 141)
Weaving in (see pages 139–140)

MAIN BODY PIECE
Cast on 131 sts using size 6 (4mm) needles.
Work in Fern Leaf patt, as follows:
Row 1 (RS): k2, *yo, k2, sl1k2togpsso, k2, yo, k1; rep from * to last st, k1.
Row 2 and every alternate row: p to end.
Row 3: K3, *yo, k1, sl1k2togpsso, k1, yo, k3; rep from * to end.
Row 5: K4, *yo, sl1, k2tog, psso, yo, k5; rep from * to last 7 sts, yo, sl1k2togpsso, yo, k4.
Row 7: K1, k2tog, *k2, yo, k1, yo, k2, sl1k2togpsso; rep from * to last 8 sts, k2, yo, k1, yo, k2, skpo, k1.
Row 9: K1, k2tog, *k1, yo, k3, yo, k1, sl1k2togpsso; rep from * to last 8 sts, k1, yo, k3, yo, k1, skpo, k1.
Row 11: K1, k2tog, *yo, k5, yo, sl1k2togpsso; rep from * to last 8 sts, yo, k5, yo, skpo, k1.
Row 12: Purl.
These 12 rows form the patt.
Rep 10 times more. Bind off.

EDGING
Cast on 8 sts using size 3 (3.25mm) needles.
Work in Scallops patt for the edging, as follows:
Row 1 (RS): sl1, k to end.
Row 2: Knit.
Row 3: Sl1, k3, ytrn, k2tog, ytrn, k2. (11 sts)
Row 4: K2, work p1 and k1 into double loop, k1, work k1 and p1 into double loop (created by ytrn in Row 3), k4.
Row 5: Sl1, k to end.
Row 6: K2, ytrn, skpo, k1, k2tog, ytrn, skpo, k2. (12 sts)
Row 7: Sl, k2, work p1 and k1 into double loop, k3, work k1 and p1 into double loop, k2.
Row 8: Knit.
Row 9: Sl1, k2, k2tog, ytrn, sl 2 as if to k2tog, K1, p2sso, ytrn, (k2tog) twice. (11 sts)
Row 10: K2, work p1 and k1 into double loop, k1, work k1 and p1 into double loop, k4.
Row 11: Sl1, k to end.
Row 12: Slipping first st, bind off 3, k to end. (8 sts)
These 12 rows form the patt.
Continue working in patt until edging, when slightly stretched, fits all round outer edge, ending row 12. Bind off.

Attaching edging
With RS together, carefully pin edging to main piece and, using a yarn needle, neatly oversew in place. Fasten off and weave in any ends.

TO FINISH
Block knitting to size. Weave in any ends.

💡 DESIGNER'S TIP

To make your gauge swatch:
Cast on 35 sts (4 pattern repeats plus 3 sts).
Work 4 rows knit.
Work rows 1–6 of main patt.
Row 7: K1, k2tog, *k2, yfd, k1, yfd, k2, sl1, k1, psso**. Attach a removable marker to the next stitch. Rep from * to ** and attach another removable stitch marker to the last stitch just worked. You will have 16sts in between the two markers. Rep from * to the end of the row.
Work rows 8–12 of the main patt, then work rows 1–12 again.
Work 4 rows knit.
To check your gauge, measure the space between the two stitch markers and the length of the swatch in between the sets of 4 knit rows. This will give the gauge.

4

KNITTING IN
THE ROUND

Learning to knit in the round opens up a whole new world of
knitting projects and patterns—socks, hats, and gloves are obvious
choices, but even larger projects such as sweaters and jackets are
all much easier to achieve when knitted this way.

Introducing knitting in the round

Hand-knitted socks and funky hats have never been more popular. Satisfying to knit, portable, and with a huge range of designs and yarns to choose from, they make learning to knit in the round an essential technique in any knitter's repertoire.

KNITTING IN THE ROUND BASICS

WHAT IS KNITTING IN THE ROUND?
Knitting in the round (also called circular knitting) describes a technique in which the work is worked in a continuous spiral, forming a tube rather than a flat fabric. It can be worked using one or two circular needles or a set of double-pointed needles (DPNs). A circular needle is simply two short needles joined by a flexible cord. Double-pointed needles come in sets of four or five needles with points at each end, which means that the work can be knitted from either end of the needle.

TOP TIPS FOR KNITTING IN THE ROUND

• As four DPNs are used at once, buy a set of five as you'll have a spare in your workbag in case you lose or break one!

• Padlock or clip-on stitch markers that can be inserted into the work are preferable for marking your place with DPNs, since they won't slip off the needles.

• Patterns will normally state whether to use four or five DPNs, circular needles, or to use the magic loop method (see page 92). In many cases, these are interchangeable, but for your first projects follow the designer's instructions. Doing this should help you to follow the pattern, since the designer may give instructions that reference the needle number.

• When working with DPNs, try different needle lengths, particularly if you find you are losing stitches. Usually around 20 stitches will fit on a short 5in. (12.5cm) DPN. If you have more stitches, the 7½in. (19cm) length may be better; some knitters prefer the longer needles for all their projects.

• Different needle materials can make knitting in the round much easier. Try wood or bamboo if stitches are dropping off the needles, as metal can be quite slippery. They also have a little flexibility, which can be useful when working with small numbers of stitches.

• When traveling, slide your work onto the cord if working on circular needles. If working with DPNs, use point protectors to stop the stitches slipping off the needles. No point protectors? A small rubber band will do the trick.

WHEN IS THIS TECHNIQUE USED AND WHY?
Knitting in the round is frequently used for projects where seams would be uncomfortable or unattractive, for example, socks, gloves, and hats. It may also be used in sweaters where a pattern may be disrupted by a seam.

WHAT ARE THE ADVANTAGES OF KNITTING IN THE ROUND?
Knitting in the round creates knitted fabrics that require minimal making up, since there are fewer seams to stitch. Because the work is never turned, the right side of the work usually faces you, making it easier to follow patterns and spot errors. The knit stitch can frequently be used throughout, which many knitters find quicker.

WHAT ARE THE DISADVANTAGES OF KNITTING IN THE ROUND?
It can be easy to lose track of where you are in a pattern, since there isn't a point where all the knitting has moved from one needle to the other. This can be avoided by using stitch markers. It can take a little longer to master holding the needles when knitting in the round, particularly with DPNs where three or four needles are being held at the same time.

CHARTS FOR KNIT IN THE ROUND PROJECTS
For projects knit in the round, each line in the chart is read in the same direction, usually starting at the bottom-right corner and reading from right to left. For more information on charts, see pages 56–59.

KEY TERMINOLOGY
When knitting on circular needles we refer to rounds rather than rows, so one completed row on a chart is one round in a circular-knitted pattern.

Using double-pointed needles

Double-pointed needles are ideal for small projects. Juggling four needles may feel awkward initially, but with practice it's a quick way to whip up a pair of socks, mitts, or a hat.

Double-pointed needles or DPNs are generally short—5in. (12.5cm) and 7¹⁄₂in. (19cm) being the most common lengths. Whether you use four or five needles is largely a matter of preference, but it is easier to use the number stated in your pattern to avoid having to make adjustments to get the right stitches on the right needles.

DPNs are needed when only a small number of stitches is being worked. They balance the work well, avoiding stretching, and some knitters find it more convenient than pushing stitches around a cable, particularly as some circular needles may have quite unwieldy cords and snaggy joins.

CASTING ON AND JOINING THE CIRCLE—FOLD AND DIVIDE METHOD

Using this method, stitches are cast on to a single DPN. They are then divided onto a second one, folded together, and the circle joined. The circle is joined at this point and the remaining stitches are divided as they are knitted rather than being slipped off onto new needles. This method makes twisting less likely.

When the stitches are divided onto the needles, you will have a "spare"

needle. This is your working needle. It will be used to join the circle and knit the next stitches. Think of it as the right needle in normal knitting, held empty in your right hand, ready to knit the next row. The four needles with stitches already on them are the equivalent of your left needle, but each of the four holds one quarter of the stitches, waiting in turn to be knitted.

STEP 1
Cast on 40 stitches onto one DPN (see page 26).

JOINING THE CIRCLE

The cast-on stitches must now be made into a circle by joining the first stitch cast on to the last.

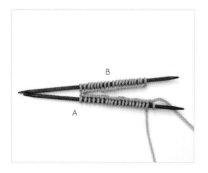

STEP 2
Slip half the stitches onto a new DPN (B). Fold the two DPNs together with the folded end at the left and the open end to the right. The working yarn is on the lower needle (A). Check carefully to ensure that the stitches aren't twisted.

STEP 3
With the closed points of (A) and (B) held together and the open points slightly apart, insert a new needle (C) into the first stitch on the left needle (B).

STEP 4
Knit this stitch off onto needle (C). Draw up the working yarn quite tightly to make a neat join.

CONTINUING KNITTING

Once the stitches have been joined, knitting continues by working the stitches from each needle in turn.

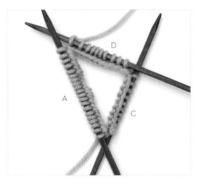

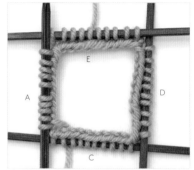

STEP 5
Knit the next nine stitches from needle (B) onto needle (C) [10 stitches]. One quarter of the stitches are now on needle (C).

STEP 6
Take a new DPN (D) and knit the remaining stitches from needle (B). This should use up all the stitches on needle (B) and you can put needle (B) aside for the moment.

STEP 7
Rotate the work clockwise and use a new DPN (E) to knit the first 10 stitches from needle (A). When rotating the work, be careful always to turn clockwise and don't turn the work over.

 CLINIC

I'VE WORKED A COUPLE OF ROUNDS BUT I CAN SEE A LADDER APPEARING WHERE I SWAP NEEDLES. WHAT SHOULD I DO?

If you notice that the stitches where you change needles are too large and look like a ladder, the first thing to do is to check that you haven't lost any stitches.

Providing your stitch numbers are correct, it most likely means that you aren't pulling the first stitch tightly enough when you change needles. It feels unnatural, but pulling quite tightly prevents ladders forming. With practice this does get easier.

DID YOU KNOW?

The Flexiknit, produced by a Norwegian company in the 1920s, is thought to be the first circular needle in commercial production. It comprised two short metal needles joined by a metal wire cord. Slow to take off in the early days, improvements in materials, smoother joins, and more flexible cords have seen circular needles embraced by knitters around the world.

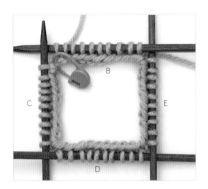

STEP 8
Rotate the work and use the empty DPN (B) to knit the remaining stitches from needle (A). Place a stitch marker here to show that each stitch has been knit. You have now worked one round. Needle (A) is empty, ready to start the next round.

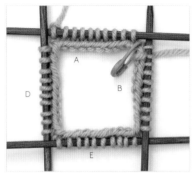

STEP 9
Rotate the needles clockwise and use the empty (working) needle (A) to knit the stitches off needle (C). (Note that the marker has rotated, too.)

STEP 10
When the needle is empty, rotate the needles clockwise again, and knit the next set of stitches off needle (D) using needle (C).

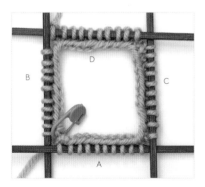

STEP 11
As needle (D) is empty, rotate the needles again and knit the stitches off needle (E).

STEP 12
When needle is (E) is empty, rotate the needles again and knit the stitches off needle (B). Round two has been completed. Repeat steps 7–10, moving the stitch marker up the work every 2–3 rounds so that it is easy to find your place.

Note that when you are knitting, the right side of the work should always be facing you. If you lose your place, squeeze the wrong side together with the needle attached to the working yarn toward you. With this needle in the right hand continue knitting.

BINDING OFF

Most of the same methods for binding off can be used when knitting with double-pointed needles. This is a simple method for a firm edge that is not too stretchy. For a stretchy alternative (handy for sock cuffs, etc.), see page 45.

STEP 1
Knit the first two stitches from the left needle as normal.

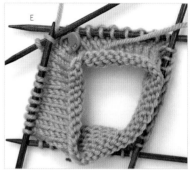

STEP 2
Use the left needle to carefully lift the first stitch knitted on needle (E) over the second stitch.

STEP 5
Repeat steps 2–4, being careful to draw up the stitches closely when moving from one needle to the next. When one stitch remains, remove the needle and draw out the stitch to form a large loop.

STEP 3
Drop the stitch off the needle. One stitch remains on needle (E).

STEP 4
Knit the next stitch. Two stitches are now on needle (E).

STEP 6
Leaving a tail of around 6in. (15cm), snip off the working yarn and pass it through the loop.

STEP 7
Draw up the loop snugly. The tail can be used for sewing up or simply darned in and trimmed (see pages 139–140).

QUICK PROJECTS FOR KNITTING IN THE ROUND

- Cozy wristwarmers are always a favorite. Choose a fine yarn for a more delicate look or for quick results and a bold look, go for a chunky yarn and big needles, and make longer "sleeves" (or even legwarmers!).

- Hats are also a great choice for knitting in the round. You may need to work on DPNs when you reach the crown.

- Once you have a little more practice, being able to knit in the round opens up the exciting world of sock knitting!

Using a circular needle

For larger projects, knitting in the round on circular needles allows the work to rest in the lap, reducing weight on your hands. Shorter cords also give scope for smaller projects.

A circular needle comprises two short needles joined by a flexible cord. Different cord lengths are available and choosing the right length of cord is important. Ideally, stitches should fit comfortably around the needles and cord, without being stretched. Some kits offer interchangeable cords and can be joined together for even longer lengths. For projects with a very small circumference, it may be necessary to change between circular needles and DPNs.

CASTING ON

With circular needles, one tip is treated as the left needle and the other as the right needle. Casting on can be done using most methods. Here, the two-needle method is being used (see page 25).

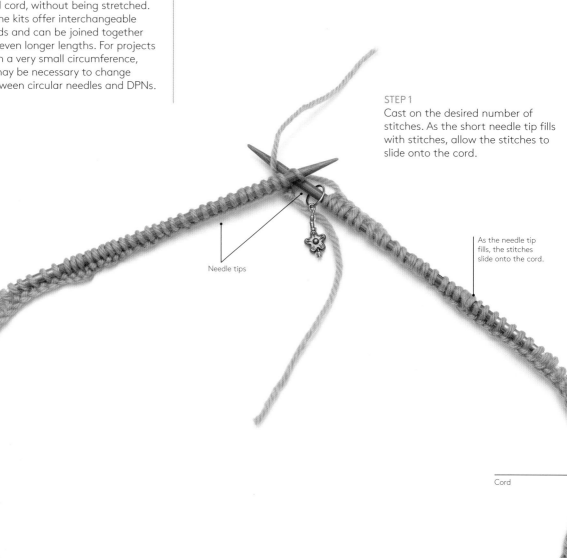

STEP 1
Cast on the desired number of stitches. As the short needle tip fills with stitches, allow the stitches to slide onto the cord.

Needle tips

As the needle tip fills, the stitches slide onto the cord.

Cord

JOINING THE CIRCLE

Once the stitches have been cast on, the work needs to be joined to form a circle.

STEP 2
Lay the work flat with the needle tips together. Place a stitch marker on the right needle tip and spread the stitches evenly around the needles and cord. Check that there are no twists in the cast-on stitches.

STEP 3
Hold the needles as normal, with the cord in between and the working yarn on the right needle. Knit the first stitch from the left needle, drawing up the yarn tightly so as not to create a hole at the join.

CONTINUING KNITTING

Once the stitches have been joined, knitting continues by working the stitches from each needle in turn.

STEP 4
Continue to knit stitches onto the right needle. As knitting progresses, shuffle stitches around the cord onto the left needle, ready to be knitted. At the same time, as the right needle fills up, allow the knitted stitches to slide onto the cord.

STEP 5
When the stitch marker is reached, this completes one round (equivalent to one row in flat knitting). This is represented by one row on a chart.

STEP 6
Once the first round has been completed, knitting can continue, following the chart or pattern. Continue knitting by first slipping the marker over to the right needle. Work the stitches on the left needle, drawing up the yarn firmly to avoid a hole, as before, shuffling the stitches off the right tip and around the cord, and easing the left stitches onto the left needle tip.

BINDING OFF

Most of the same methods for binding off can be used with circular needles. This is a classic bind off. For a stretchy alternative (handy for sock cuffs, etc.), see page 45.

STEP 1
Knit the first two stitches from the left needle as normal.

STEP 2
Use the left needle tip to lift the first stitch over the second stitch.

 CLINIC

I'M KNITTING A HAT BUT STRUGGLING TO STRETCH THE STITCHES ALL THE WAY AROUND THE CORD. WHAT SHOULD I DO?

- When knitting in the round on circular needles, getting the right cord length is important. If you are not using the magic loop method (see page 92), your cord should be just long enough for the cast-on stitches to reach all the way round, filling the cord and the needle tips (see page 88).
- When the cord is too short, the stitches will have to be stretched when the work is moved around the circle. Not only can this distort the knitting, but it's also quite uncomfortable to wrestle with stitches that are over-stretched!
- If you have an interchangeable set, try a shorter cord. Alternatively, if your cord is too long, try the magic loop method as that works best with longer cords.

STEP 5
Repeat steps 2–4, being careful to draw up the stitches closely when moving from one needle to the next.

STEP 6
When one stitch remains, remove the needle and draw out the stitch to form a large loop.

STEP 3
Drop the stitch off the needle.

STEP 4
Knit the next stitch.

STEP 7
Leaving a tail of around 6in. (15cm), snip off the working yarn and pass it through the loop.

STEP 8
Draw up the loop snugly. The tail can be used for sewing up or simply darned in and trimmed (see pages 139–140).

CARING FOR YOUR NEEDLES

- Keep your circular needles somewhere safe. The flexible cords can be easily damaged or will develop bends or creases if stored at the bottom of a bag. A flat pouch with pockets for each needle is ideal.

- When cables get very bent, it may be possible to reshape them by dipping in hot water and allowing the plastic to soften a little. Straighten gently under the water, but don't allow the tips or joins to get wet. Hang to dry straight.

- Keep needle tips and cords in good condition by cleaning them regularly with a soft, lint-free cloth. Over time, hand creams, perfumes, and being in your knitting bag can make cords less slippery, so an occasional buff will do wonders. Check the joins for snags and think about replacing any damaged needles.

The magic loop method

The magic loop method allows projects to be knit in the round, even where there is only a small number of stitches. It is a particularly popular technique for sock knitting and uses a single circular needle.

CASTING ON

Magic loop is the perfect combination for knitters who want to make smaller projects, but prefer a circular needle to DPNs. This is a great technique for sock knitting.

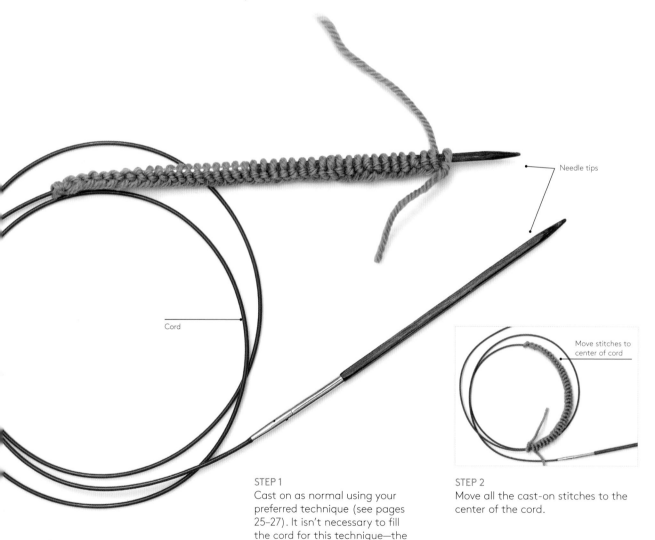

Needle tips

Cord

Move stitches to center of cord

STEP 1
Cast on as normal using your preferred technique (see pages 25–27). It isn't necessary to fill the cord for this technique—the empty length of cord forms part of the method.

STEP 2
Move all the cast-on stitches to the center of the cord.

JOINING THE CIRCLE

Once the stitches have been cast on, in order to knit in the round they have to be joined into a circle to continue knitting.

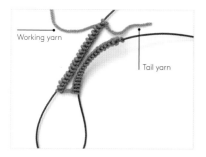

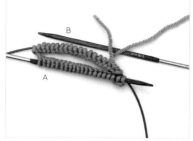

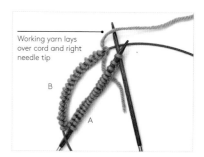

STEP 3
With the working yarn to the right, fold the cord in half, dividing the stitches into two roughly equal groups. Pinch the cord and pull the center of the cord away from the tips so that half the stitches are on each side of the cord with a loop to the left. The working yarn should be attached to the back group of stitches.

STEP 4
With the loop on the left and the needle tips on the right, half the stitches—the front group (A)—are closer to you, while the other group—the back group (B)—is farther away from you. Holding both groups of stitches, carefully ease the front stitches (A) onto the front needle by drawing the front loop out to the left. Draw the back needle to the right until the back group of stitches (B) are roughly in the middle of the cord. Bring the back needle tip to meet the tip of the front needle.

STEP 5
Insert the empty needle tip into the first stitch on the front group (A). Then, making sure that the working yarn is coming from below the back needle, bring it up in between the needle tips and rest it over the top of the back needle. Check that the cast-on stitches are not twisted.

STEP 6
Knit into the first stitch of the front group (A). Draw up the yarn tightly to join the yarn into a circle and avoid a gap where the stitches join.

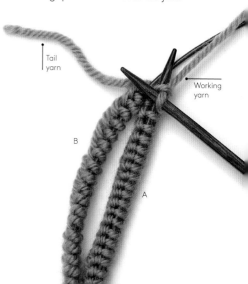

 CLINIC

I'M KNITTING IN THE ROUND FOR A COLORWORK PROJECT AND MY KNITTING SEEMS TO BE PULLING IN THE MORE I KNIT. IS THERE A WAY TO AVOID THIS HAPPENING?

Knitting to the correct gauge is always important in colorwork, but even more so with knitting in the round. Usually, the tricky spots are when "floats" (the yarns being carried across the back of the work) are moved around the needles.

Where possible, avoid stretching long color changes across the needles. Work to the stitch before the color change and weave in the final stitch. Change color on the next stitch, then move the stitches around the needles. Working in this way means that there may be more weaving in (see pages 139–140), but ensures that the floats are as short as possible.

Check the gauge of your floats regularly by carefully stretching out the stitches a little. There should be enough stretch to allow, for example, a foot to go into a sock or an arm to go down a sleeve.

CONTINUING KNITTING

Once the stitches have been joined, knitting continues by working the stitches from each needle in turn.

STEP 7
Continue knitting the front group (A) of stitches.

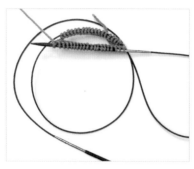

STEP 8
When all the stitches in the front group have been worked, the stitches you have just worked are in your right hand and the tip of the needle is pointing to the left. The loop of the cord is on the right and the "open" cord is on the left.

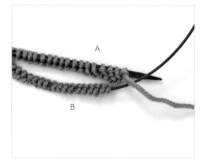

STEP 9
Bring the working yarn above the cord and rotate the needles. The stitches just worked (A) are now at the back and the tip of the needle points to the right. The unworked stitches (B) are on the cord at the front. The open cord is on the right.

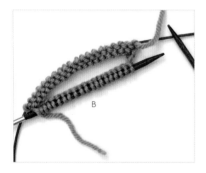

STEP 10
Slide the front stitches (B) along the cord and onto the empty needle tip by pulling out the cord to the left. A loop will form on the left.

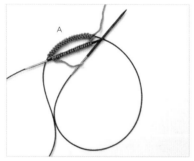

STEP 11
Slide the back stitches (A) onto the center of the cord. You should have a loop on the left and an empty tip and open cord on the right.

STEP 12
Use the empty tip to knit the stitches (B) off the front needle. When all the stitches have been knitted, the full needle tip points to the left.

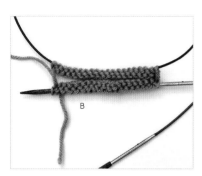

STEP 13
When all the stitches (B) have been worked, you will have completed one round of knitting.

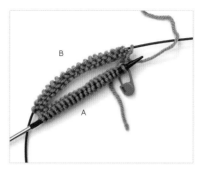

STEP 14
Place a marker here to indicate the start of the round. Ensuring that the working yarn is above the needles, rotate the needles so that the (A) stitches are at the front and the (B) stitches at the back. Slide the (A) stitches onto the needle. Pull out the needle so that the (B) stitches sit on the cord. Repeat steps 7–15, moving the stitch marker every row to indicate the start of the round.

STEP 15
When you put your knitting away, store it on the loop.

STEP 16
When you are ready to start knitting again, squeeze the WS together, place the working yarn to the back, and slide the front stitches back onto the needle. Slide the back stitches onto the cord.

 TOP TIPS FOR MASTERING MAGIC LOOP

- When using interchangeable needles, keep a close eye on the join between the tip and the cord. If the needle manufacturer supplies a tightening key (many do), use the key and retighten every round to prevent the two sections coming apart.

- Working with magic loop requires a long cord (at least 31in./80cm) and a soft cord that can be easily manipulated. It is worth trying out different brands as some cords behave better than others!

- If in doubt when selecting the cords for magic-loop knitting, go for a longer length. If the cord is too short, it will make it more difficult to form the loops on either side. Longer cords mean larger loops, but with a soft cord this isn't usually an issue.

- If you find that your cord is too short and you don't have an alternative, try pulling a single loop to one side rather than two loops.

BINDING OFF

Most of the same methods for binding off can be used with magic loop. This is a classic bind off. For a stretchy alternative (handy for sock cuffs, etc.), see page 45.

STEP 1
Knit the first two stitches from the left needle as normal.

STEP 2
Use the left needle tip to lift the first stitch over the second stitch.

STEP 3
Drop the stitch off the needle.

 CLINIC

MY FINISHED SOCKS LOOK GREAT, BUT THE BIND OFF IS SO TIGHT I DON'T THINK I'LL BE ABLE TO PUT THEM ON.

When binding off, it's important to consider the needs of the project. If you are knitting socks, hats, or sleeve cuffs, you'll need a stretchy bind off. You may also need a stretchy cast on (depending on whether the pieces are knit from the bottom up or the top down). For a neat but forgiving cast on and cast off, try the extra-stretchy version shown on page 45.

If you've already bound off, you should be able to undo the tail and take back the bind off to rework it. If your tail is very short, take back a couple of rounds and join in the working yarn again, as otherwise you may not have enough yarn (stretchy bind offs use more yarn). Joining a new yarn on the cast-off row can look untidy and may not be secure enough to stand up to wear and tear.

STEP 6
Leaving a tail of around 6in. (15cm), snip off the working yarn and pass it through the loop.

STEP 7
Draw up the loop snugly. The tail can be used for sewing up or simply darned in and trimmed (see pages 139–140).

STEP 5
Repeat steps 2–4, being careful to draw up the stitches closely when moving from one needle to the next. When one stitch remains, remove the needle and draw out the stitch to form a large loop.

STEP 4
Knit the next stitch.

 ## TOP TIPS FOR CIRCULAR NEEDLES

- When turning the work, it's easy to accidentally create an extra stitch by wrapping the yarn around the cord. Avoid this by making sure the working yarn is above and away from the cord before you turn the work.

- When choosing needles for magic loop, aim for a cord that is soft with good flexibility. Some types have a swivel where the tip joins the cord, which some knitters find helpful. With interchangeable needles, check how the cord attaches to the tip—some types have a screw thread which is tightened with a little key. Others have a click mechanism. Depending on your knitting style, you may find that one type works better for you than the other, so, if you can, buy one before investing in a whole set (or borrow from a fellow knitter). This may save frustration (and money) in the long run.

- Keep cords clean as the plastic can attract dust and dirt over time and your stitches won't slide smoothly. A wipe with a clean, lint-free cloth is usually sufficient, but a tiny amount of soapy water is okay as long as you avoid the metal parts that may rust if wet.

- Stitch markers are a "must-have" for knitting in the round, especially with magic loop, as it's more difficult to work out where the end of a round is. However, if you don't have stitch markers, make a slip knot in a small loop of spare yarn and pop it over the needle—it will work just fine.

Knitting in the round

BE INSPIRED

1. HAT
This is a simple hat by Kim Hargreaves that would make a great first striping-in-the-round project. Lovely, chunky wool would make it a quick, satisfying knit.

2. FOX SOCKS
Who could resist these cute foxy socks? An intermediate knitter ready to get into a little bit of colorwork alongside knitting in the round would find these socks by Susanna Mertsalmi fun to knit.

3

4

3. COWL

Cowls are great for wintery weather when you need something snug that won't fly around in the breeze! Knit in the round with an interesting, open-stitch pattern, this cowl by Quail Studio would make an ideal project for an intermediate knitter trying their first circular knit project.

4. MITTS

A project for the more advanced knitter, these colorwork mitts by Arne & Carlos are knit in the round. The pairing of a monochrome Fair Isle with the colorful stripe cuffs makes a great combination.

Quick start project

Tubular ski socks

These socks do not have a heel, which makes them a great introduction to working on double-pointed needles because you can just concentrate on mastering working in the round. The socks use only knit and purl stitches, and the spiral is created by moving the rib along after every fourth round.

FINISHED SIZE
To fit the approximate shoe sizes:
Small: US shoe sizes, approximately 4–6 (UK 2–4; European 35–37)
Medium: US shoe sizes, approximately 6–8 (UK 4–6; European 37–39)
Large: US shoe sizes, approximately 8–10 (UK 6–8; European 39–41)

GAUGE
Yarn used knits as DK to this gauge:
26 sts and 40 rows = 4in. (10cm) square using size 3 (3.25mm) DPNs over spiral rib stitch

YOU WILL NEED
- 1 x 2oz (50g) ball of DK weight yarn in color A
- 1 x 2oz (50g) ball of DK weight yarn in color B
  (You'll need about 220yd/200m in total for a pair of average-length ankle socks); Debbie knitted with Cascade 220 100% superwash wool DK, with approximately 220yd (200m) per ball, in the following shades (although any DK yarn can be substituted):
  o Color A—Hyacinth (814)
  o Color B—Sterling Blue (279)
- Size 3 (3.25mm) x 5 double-pointed needle set
- Yarn needle (for sewing up)

ABBREVIATIONS AND TECHNIQUES
DPN(s): double-pointed needle(s)
k: knit (see page 28)
p: purl (see page 30)
rep: repeat
rnd(s): round(s)
st(s): stitch(es)
Seaming (see pages 136–138)
Weaving in (see pages 139–140)

PATTERN NOTES
**Sizing note:
The length of your sock can easily be adjusted to fit. Simply repeat pattern rounds 1–16 until your sock measures 1 (1¹/₄: 1¹/₂) in./ 2.5 (3: 4) cm shorter than the desired length from the cuff to the big toe, then shape for the toe as above. When measuring, measure from the top of the desired cuff height, down the back of the heel to the floor. Then measure from the center back of the heel along the inner edge of the foot, to the tip of the big toe. Add these two together, then deduct the amount for the toe shaping. This will give you the length of tube needed before you begin shaping for the toe.

SOCK ONE
Cast on 48 (52: 60) sts using color A and size 3 (3.25mm) DPNs.
Divide the stitches by transferring them onto 2 needles (24: [28: 30] sts per needle)

Join the work into a circle (see page 83).
Complete the first round by knitting off 12 (13: 15) sts per needle (see pages 84–85).

CUFF
Mark the start of the round with a piece of waste yarn and continue knitting in the round, as follows:
Rounds 2–14: *K3, p1; rep from * to end.

LEG AND FOOT
Now work in the following spiral rib stitch and, at the same time, work in stripe sequence of 12 rounds color B, 10 rounds color A, 8 rounds color B, 6 rounds color A, 4 rounds color B, 4 rounds color A, 6 rounds color B, 8 rounds color A, 10 rounds color B, 12 rounds color A. These 80 rounds make up the stripe sequence.
Rnds 1–4: *P1, k3; rep from * to end of round.
Rnds 5–8: *K1, p1, k2; rep from * to end of round.
Rnds 9–12: *K2, p1, k1; rep from * to end of round.
Rnds 13–16: *K3, p1; rep from * to end of round.
These 16 rounds make up one pattern repeat of spiral rib stitch.
Keeping spiral rib and stripe sequence correct, continue until your knitting measures 12¹/₂ (16: 18¹/₂)in./ 32 (41: 47)cm from cast-on edge. (For re-sizing, see note ** left.)

SHAPE TOE
Size small
Rnd 1: *K1, k2tog, k3, k2tog; rep from * to end. (36 sts)
Rnds 2–3: Knit.
Rnd 4: *K2, k2tog; rep from * to end. (27 sts)
Rnds 5–6: Knit.
Rnd 7: *K1, k2tog; rep from * to end. (18 sts)
Rnds 8–9: Knit.
Rnd 10: *K2tog; rep from * to end. (9 sts)

Size medium
Rnd 1: *K3, k2tog, k3, k2tog, k3; rep from* to end.
(44 sts)
Rnds 2–3: Knit.
Rnd 4: *K2, k2tog, k3, k2tog, k2; rep from * to end.
(36 sts)
Rnds 5–6: Knit
Rnd 7: *K2, k2tog; rep from * to end. (27 sts)
Rnds 8–9: Knit
Rnd 10: *K1, k2tog; rep from * to end. (18 sts)
Rnd 11: Knit
Rnd 12: *K2tog; rep from * to end. (9 sts)

Size large
Rnd 1: *K4, k2tog, k8, k2tog, k4; rep from * to end.
(54 sts)
Rnds 2–3: Knit
Rnd 4: *K1, k2tog, k3; rep from * to end. (45 sts)
Rnds 5–6: Knit
Rnd 7: *K1, k2tog, k2; rep from * to end. (36 sts)
Rnds 8–9: Knit.
Rnd 10: *K2, k2tog; rep from * to end. (27 sts)
Rnds 11–12: Knit.
Rnd 13: *K1, k2tog; rep from * to end. (18 sts)
Rnds 14–15: Knit.
Rnd 16: *K2tog; rep from * to end. (9 sts)

All sizes: Break off yarn, leaving long tail, thread through
stitches on needles, and then draw up tightly. Fasten off
by using a yarn needle to take the tail through the
stitches and down through the center to the wrong side
of the work.

TO FINISH
Neatly weave in any ends.

SOCK TWO
Work as for sock one, but swap the colors so that where
the pattern starts to use color A, instead use color B,
and where the pattern starts to use color B, instead use
color A.

Guest Designer Jacinta Bowie

I am a knitwear and crochet designer who began working in the craft industry while at college in the 1980s. I worked as an in-house knitwear designer and I later managed one of the flagship Rowan stores in Leeds while designing editorials for them. I moved into fashion after working for the United Nations, setting up a knitwear course in New Delhi, India, in 1992. After many years globe-trotting, but always taking my knitting and crochet projects along, an illness brought me back to my first love: knitting. That was in 2005, and since then I have worked with yarn companies and magazines on many varied knitting and crochet projects. I have a passion for wool and sustainable yarns, and focus on working sustainably as much as possible. You can see my work on Instagram @Jacintabowietextiles and at www.jacintabowie.com.

Knitted baskets

Baskets are fun to make, practical, and a stylish addition to your home. Using slightly smaller needles than normal and a yarn without too much stretch will keep them sturdy.

FINISHED SIZE
Stocking-stitch basket
4½in. (11.5cm) deep, 6¼in. (16cm) diameter
Garter-stitch basket
4¾in. (12cm) deep, 7in. (18cm) diameter
Seed-stitch basket
6in. (15cm) deep, 8¾in. (22cm) diameter

GAUGE
Before felting:
11 sts and 20 rows = 4in. (10cm) square over garter stitch
11 sts and 13 rows = 4in. (10cm) square over stockinette stitch
10 sts and 13 rows = 4in. (10cm) square over seed stitch

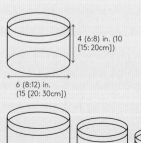

4 (6:8) in. (10 [15: 20cm])

6 (8:12) in. (15 [20: 30cm])

YOU WILL NEED
• 1 x 7oz (200g) skein of wool per basket; Jacinta knitted with Wool Couture's Cheeky Chunky 100% Merino Wool yarn, with approximately 142yd (130m) per ball, in the following three shades (if you wish to substitute, it needs to be a yarn that felts and has a high wool content):
  o Small basket—Mink
  o Medium basket—Seal
  o Large basket—Granite
• Size 11 (8mm) circular needle, 15¾in. (40cm) long
• Size 11 (8mm) x 5 double-pointed needle set, 6in. (15cm) long
• Stitch marker
• Yarn needle (for sewing up)

ABBREVIATIONS AND TECHNIQUES
alt: alternate
DPN: double-pointed needle
foll: follow(s)(ing)
k: knit (see page 28)
k2tog: knit two together
p: purl (see page 30)
rep: repeat
rnd(s): round(s)
sm: slip marker
st(s): stitch(es)
st st: stocking stitch, every round knit
Weaving in (see pages 139–140)

SMALL STOCKING-STITCH BASKET (MINK)
Cast on 56 sts using size 11 (8mm) 15¾in. (40cm) circular needle and the two-needle cast-on method (see pages 88–89).

Place a stitch marker on the needle to denote the beginning and end of each round.
Taking care not to let the stitches twist on the needle, so you end up with a spiral instead of a tube, work in the round. Knit into the first cast-on stitch to make sure you are working in the round.
Rnd 1: Knit to end, sm.
Rnd 2: Purl to end, sm.
Rep last two rnds 3 times altogether.
Now continue in st st (every rnd knit) for 16 rnds more.
Work in garter stitch for base hem, as follows:
Rnd 1: Purl to end, sm.
Rnd 2: Knit to end, sm.
Rep last two rnds twice more.
Next Rnd: Purl to end.

SHAPING FOR BASE
Rnd 1: *K5, k2tog; rep from * to end, sm. (48 sts)
Rnd 2 and every foll alt rnd: Purl to end, sm.
Rnd 3: Knit to end, sm.
Rnd 5: *K4, k2tog; rep from * to end, sm. (40 sts)
Rnd 7: *K3, k2tog; rep from * to end, sm. (32 sts)
Rnd 9: *K2, k2tog; rep from * to end, sm. (24 sts)
Now working on DPN, split the stitches evenly onto four needles and work with the fifth needle.
Rnd 11: *K1, k2tog; rep from * to end, sm. (16 sts)
Rnd 13: *K2tog; rep from * to end. (8 sts)
Rnd 14: Purl to end.
Break off yarn, draw through remaining sts, and fasten off.

MEDIUM GARTER-STITCH BASKET (SEAL)

Cast on 64 sts using size 11 (8mm) 15¾in. (40cm) circular needle (see pages 88–89).

Place a stitch marker on the needle to denote the beginning and end of each round.

Taking care not to let the stitches twist on the needle, so you end up with a spiral instead of a tube, work in the round. Knit into the first cast-on stitch to make sure you are working in the round.

Rnd 1: Knit to end, sm.
Rnd 2: Purl to end, sm.
Rep last two rnds 15 times altogether.

SHAPING FOR BASE

Rnd 1: *K6, k2tog; rep from * to end, sm. (56 sts)
Rnd 2 and every foll alt rnd: Purl to end, sm.
Rnd 3: Knit to end, sm.
Rnd 5: *K5, k2tog; rep from * to end, sm. (48 sts)
Rnd 7: *K4, k2tog; rep from * to end, sm. (40 sts)
Rnd 9: *K3, k2tog; rep from * to end, sm. (32 sts)
Now working on DPN, split the stitches evenly onto four needles and work with the fifth needle.
Rnd 11: *K2, k2tog; rep from * to end, sm. (24 sts)
Rnd 13: *K1, k2tog; rep from * to end, sm. (16 sts)
Rnd 15: *K2tog; rep from * to end. (8 sts)
Rnd 16: Purl to end.
Break off yarn, draw through remaining sts, and fasten off.

LARGE SEED-STITCH BASKET (GRANITE)

Cast on 72 sts using size 11 (8mm) 15¾in. (40cm) circular needle (see pages 88–89).

Place a stitch marker on the needle to denote the beginning and end of each round.

Taking care not to let the stitches twist on the needle, so you end up with a spiral instead of a tube, work in the round. Knit into the first cast-on stitch to make sure you are working in the round.

Rnd 1: Knit to end, sm.
Rnd 2: Purl to end, sm.
Rep last two rnds twice more.
Now continue in seed-stitch pattern, as follows:

SEED-STITCH PATTERN

Rnd 1: *K1, p1; rep from * to end, sm.
Rnd 2: *P1, k1; rep from * to end, sm.
Rep last two rnds 15 times altogether.

HEM PATTERN

Rnd 1: Purl to end, sm.
Rnd 2: Knit to end, sm.
Rep last two rnds once more.
Next rnd: Purl to end.
Work shaping for base hem, as follows:
Rnd 1: *K7, k2tog; rep from * to end, sm. (64 sts)
Rnd 2 and every foll alt rnd: Purl to end, sm.
Rnd 3: Knit to end, sm.
Rnd 5: *K6, k2tog; rep from * to end, sm. (56 sts)
Rnd 7: *K5, k2tog; rep from * to end, sm. (48 sts)

Rnd 9: *K4, k2tog; rep from * to end, sm. (40 sts)
Rnd 11: *K3, k2tog; rep from * to end, sm. (32 sts)
Now working on DPNs, split the sts evenly onto four needles and work with the fifth needle.
Rnd 13: *K2, k2tog; rep from * to end, sm. (24 sts)
Rnd 15: *K1, k2tog; rep from * to end, sm. (16 sts)
Rnd 17: K2tog; rep from * to end. (8 sts)
Rnd 18: Purl to end.
Break off yarn, draw through remaining sts, and fasten off.

TO MAKE UP ALL BASKETS

1. Weave in the tail at the cast-on and fasten-off points, then trim.
2. Place each basket in the washing machine on its own without detergent and wash on a short cycle at 104°F (40°C) to felt the yarn. This will firm up the fabric and make the baskets more sturdy.
3. Pull to shape and let dry over a vessel that's a similar size and shape as each basket (if available), removing excess fibers beforehand.

5

COLORWORK

Colorwork knitting looks amazing, although it can seem daunting
to the beginner. However, stripes are surprisingly easy to master,
and even Fair Isle and intarsia are within the reach of a new knitter
if you follow these simple techniques and our handy tips.

Working stripes

Whether you are looking for bold contrasts or subtle enhancements, stripes can quickly turn a simple knit into something special.

WORKING STRIPES IN FLAT KNITTING

In flat knitting, a two-row stripe is the simplest option. It is easy to switch from one color to another, and by working with an even number of rows the yarn should always end at the same side of the work, ready to start with the new color. Wider stripes and odd-row numbers are also possible, of course, with just a couple of little tweaks.

WORKING TWO-ROW STRIPES
Two-row stripes are the easiest way to begin since they require only a single modification to your normal knitting every two rows.

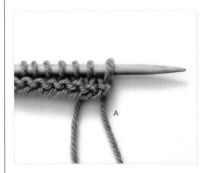

STEP 1
For a two-row stripe, work the first two rows in color A as normal.

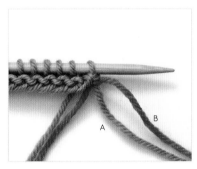

STEP 2
When you are ready to join in a new color, don't break off color A. Instead, leaving a 4in. (10cm) tail of color B, hold A and B together and knot color B to color A. Don't make the knot too tight, as you will need to undo it later, and make the knot as close to the edge of the work as possible to keep the gauge even.

CLINIC

I'M KNITTING A SWEATER IN RED AND WHITE STRIPES, AND NOW I'M WORRIED IN CASE THE COLORS RUN. IS THERE ANYTHING I CAN DO?

Even with the best yarn, it's always possible that two colors (especially very strong colors) can run in the wash. To save disappointment, when you are making your gauge swatch you should wash and block it too. This should highlight any potential issues. Wash the swatch as you will when it's being used—if it will be machine-washed, throw it in the machine!

If it's already knit, there may not be much you can do; however, you can try the following: Do an initial wash by hand in cold water with no detergent. Swirl the garment in plenty of water, drain off most of the water, and then gently roll the garment in a large towel rather than squeezing, to remove the excess water. Repeat if required. If there is color coming out,

a "color catcher" cloth in the water may help. Once you've done a couple of cold washes, a detergent like Synthrapol is a good option as it is designed to catch stray dye molecules and prevent them from reattaching to the fibers. It's mainly used in hand dyeing, so try a dye supplier or craft store.

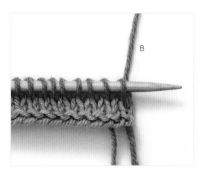

STEP 3
Work the next two rows in color B.

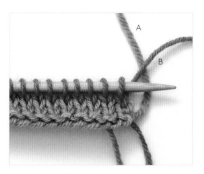

STEP 4
To swap over colors, bring color A up behind B and drop color B.

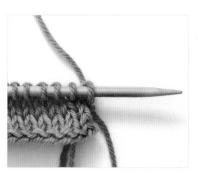

STEP 5
Keeping an even gauge, continue to knit, working two rows with color A.

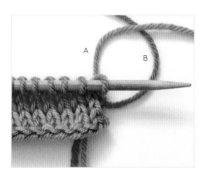

STEP 6
Bring color B up behind colour A, and drop yarn A.

STEP 7
Work two more rows.

STEP 8
When you have finished with a color, work to the end of the row and cut off the yarn, leaving a 4in. (10cm) tail for weaving in later.

When you are ready to bring in a new color, repeat step 2.

When you have finished your knitting, carefully weave in any ends (see pages 139–140).

WORKING FOUR-ROW STRIPES

Four-row stripes need just a little extra tweak as the yarns are twisted every couple of rows to carry them up the side of the fabric until they are needed. This avoids long strands that can affect the tension of the fabric and catch in fingers.

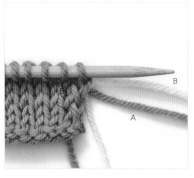

STEP 1
For a stripe of four rows (or more), work the required number of rows in color A as normal.

STEP 2
When you are ready to join in a new color, don't break off color A. Instead, leaving a 4in. (10cm) tail of color B, hold A and B together, and knot color B to color A. Don't make the knot too tight, as you will need to undo it later, and make the knot as close to the edge of the work as possible to keep the gauge even.

STEP 3
Work the next two rows in color B.

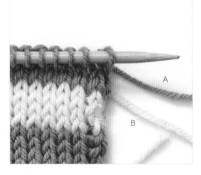

STEP 4
Even though you are continuing to work in color B, you will need to wrap the yarns at the edge of the work to prevent long, loose strands, so bring color A up behind B. Take A under B, effectively wrapping A around B. Continue to knit with color B. Repeat this process, wrapping the unused yarn around the working yarn every two rows.

STEP 5
To change colors, bring color A up behind color A, wrap it around B, and then drop color B.

STEP 6
Continue to knit in A, wrapping color B every two rows. When you have finished with a color, work to the end of the row and cut off the yarn, leaving a 4in. (10cm) tail for weaving in later.

When you are ready to bring in a new color, repeat step 2.

When you have finished your knitting, carefully weave in any ends (see pages 139–140).

ODD-ROW STRIPES

Where a pattern is knit flat, but has an odd number of rows, the same process applies as for other stripes. Sometimes it may be possible to work with several small balls of yarn that are left in place and wrapped up the edge of the knitting until needed. Alternatively, the yarn must be cut and rejoined at each end, as shown.

WORKING STRIPES IN THE ROUND

Working stripes in the round is very similar to working stripes in flat knitting with two key exceptions:
- It is possible to work both odd and even numbers of stripes in the same way, since the yarn is always in the correct place at the start of every round.
- When moving from one color to another, there can be a small step or "jog," so a small tweak is needed to make this less noticeable.

STEP 1
Work the required number of rows in color A as normal.

STEP 2
When you are ready to join in a new color, don't break off color A. Instead, leaving a 4in. (10cm) tail of color B, hold A and B together, and knot color B to color A. Don't make the knot too tight, as you will need to undo it later, and make the knot as close to the edge of the work as possible to keep the gauge even.

STEP 3
Work the next two rounds in color B.

STEP 4
To change colors, bring color A up behind color A and wrap it around B.

STEP 5
Work the next two rounds in color A.

STEP 6
If you are continuing to work in A, you will need to wrap the yarns at the edge of the work to prevent long, loose strands, so bring color A up behind B. Take A under B, effectively wrapping A around B. Continue knitting in A, wrapping the unused yarn around the working yarn every two rows.

AVOIDING A STEP OR "JOG" AT THE COLOR CHANGE

As knitting in the round is effectively a spiral tube rather than individual rows, where the colors change can create a small step, also referred to as a "jog." You can make this less obvious by making your color changes as follows:

Work steps 1–3 as on page 109.

STEP 4
To change colors, place a marker on the needle at the change point.

STEP 5
Knit the next stitch using colors A and B.

STEP 6
Continue knitting the rest of the round in color B. At the marker, move it to the back needle as normal (or the right needle if you are working on DPNs). You should now see that the next stitch is made up of two strands, one of color A and one of color B.

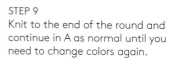

STEP 9
Knit to the end of the round and continue in A as normal until you need to change colors again.

STEP 7
If your pattern continues in color B, continue knitting in B until the next color change.

STEP 8
To change to color A, slip the marker and knit the first stitch using both A and B.

Jogless technique makes the color change less visible.

Color change without jogless stripe technique.

To change between colors, repeat steps 5–9, remembering to wrap the yarns every two rounds if you are working more than two rounds in a particular color. This prevents the yarns pulling up too tightly or loosely between color changes when working in wider stripes.

When you have finished with a color, work to the end of the round and cut off the yarn, leaving a 4in. (10cm) tail for weaving in later.

When you are ready to bring in a new color, repeat step 2.

When you have finished your knitting, carefully weave in any tails (see pages 139–140).

CLINIC

AS I MAKE MY COLOR CHANGES WHEN I'M KNITTING IN THE ROUND, I CAN SEE THE OLD COLOR. IS THERE ANYTHING I CAN DO?

- If you pull the old yarn back slightly when you make the color change this will reduce the appearance of the jog even further and should give a nice, neat changeover.
- Careful blocking will even out some of the jog effect but, where possible, locate ends of rounds in the least noticeable area, for example, at the underarm sides of a garment or up the inside edge of a sock.

Fair Isle colorwork

In Fair Isle, usually only two colors are used in one row. The unused yarn is carried across the work by "stranding" or "weaving in."

FOLLOWING FAIR ISLE CHARTS

In colorwork, each square on the chart represents a stitch. The colors on the chart normally reflect the different colors in the knitting. Of course, it isn't necessary to use the same colors when working your knitting—just be sure to make a note of which yarn color is represented by the printed color on the chart.

FLAT KNITTING

When knitting flat, charts are normally followed starting at the bottom-right corner, working from right to left on the first row, working back from left to right on row 2 (see chart on page 56). The right side of the work will normally be represented by the odd rows, even rows being worked as wrong-side rows. Where this is not the case, it will be indicated in patterns.

KNITTING IN THE ROUND

When knitting in the round, charts also start at the bottom-right edge (see chart on page 56). However, as knitting in the round is effectively knitting in a continuous spiral, every round begins at the right-hand edge with each row on the chart representing a round of knitting.

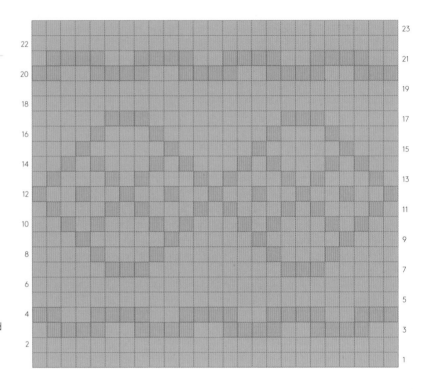

 Color A
RS row: Knit, WS row: Purl

Color B
RS row: Knit, WS row: Purl

✚ CLINIC

MY KNITTING KEEPS PULLING IN WHEN I'M STRANDING MY YARNS. WHAT SHOULD I DO?

In colorwork it's important to check the floats regularly for the correct gauge. As a general guide, floats should have enough "give" to allow the fabric to stretch and should not pull the fabric in. Test this regularly by gently stretching the fabric (at least every row) during working. If the fabric is pulling in, take the work back and re-knit, just easing a little on the float yarn to give it a bit more room to stretch.

COLORWORK TERMINOLOGY

Colorwork is a catch-all term that includes stripes, Fair Isle (stranded colorwork), and intarsia.

Fair Isle describes a traditional Scottish knitting style originating in the Shetland Islands. It is, however, often used to apply more broadly to stranded colorwork patterns. In true Fair Isle, numerous colors may be used, but only two colors are typically worked in a given row. In other parts of the world, rich colorwork traditions also exist—Selbu and Setesdal from Norway, Lopapeysa from Iceland, and the vibrant designs of the Andes and Peru, to name just a few.

Intarsia is, by contrast, not a stranded knitting style (see page 122). It's primarily used in motifs and designs where larger blocks of color are required. It is also used where small motifs are placed some distance apart when stranding would be impractical.

Key concepts in colorwork include: floats, stranding, and weaving in.

Floats describe the short lengths of yarn that occur behind the work where it is looped between stretches of two colors. Floats are anchored using either stranding or weaving in.

Stranding is where the yarn is held at the back of the work and simply looped between two colors as and when the colors are changed.

Weaving in, on the other hand, is used where the gap between two color changes is too long to be done as a single loop behind the work. In this situation, the yarn is caught in every two or three stitches to prevent long, loose loops.

In the sample on the right, seen from the wrong side, the bottom and top bands of color are worked using the stranding technique as there are only two or three stitches between color changes. In the center band, weaving in has been used as there are up to eleven stitches in some of the color sections. This is too long for a float, which could distort the fabric or catch in fingers or toes. The stranded section is a little softer when handled than where the weaving-in technique has been used. However, when seen from the right side, there should be little difference in appearance, whether the yarn has been stranded or woven in.

Wrong side

Right side

STRANDING ON A KNIT ROW

This method works well where color changes are frequent (no more than four or five stitches apart). It gives a less dense, lighter fabric than weaving in (see opposite) and uses less yarn.

STEP 1
Starting at the bottom right of the chart on page 112 and working from right to left, knit with color A until the first color change. Don't break off color A. Leave a 4in. (10cm) tail of color B, hold A and B together, and knot color B to color A, as close to the edge of the work as possible, but not too tight as you will undo this later.

STEP 2
To change to B, keeping the gauge on both yarns equal, bring color B from underneath A and knit with B. Do not pull color A tight as the float needs to be loose without being droopy.

STEP 3
Knit in B until the next color change.

STEP 4
To change back to A, bring up color A from behind B. Still keeping the gauge equal, repeat step 1 with color A in front of color B. Ensure that B is neither too tight nor too droopy. It should just rest comfortably and not pull the knitting in.

STEP 5
Knit with color A until the next color change on the chart.

STEP 6
Repeat this process, changing yarns according to the chart until the end of the row. At the end of the row, if this method has been used correctly, the yarns should not be tangled. Check that when the fabric is slightly stretched, the floats are not pulling it in.

STRANDING ON A PURL ROW

Work the next row of the chart from right to left in purl. As with the knit row, the new color is lifted from beneath the working yarn at each color change, laying the old yarn in front of the new yarn as it faces you.

STEP 1
As the first row ended with color A and row 2 begins with color B, lift color B from beneath color A. Work in B to the color change.

STEP 2
At the color change, bring color A up from under color B and make the next stitch with color A. Again, the yarns should not be twisted and the floats kept loose.

STEP 3
Using these two steps, complete row 2, following the colors as indicated on the chart.

WEAVING IN ON A KNIT ROW

For firmer fabrics, or where the floats would be too long or where even short floats would be likely to snag, weaving in may be preferable. With socks or gloves, the floats may catch on rings or between toes. This can be annoying and may spoil your knitting, so in these instances, weaving in may be the better method for changing colors within the row.

KNIT ROW

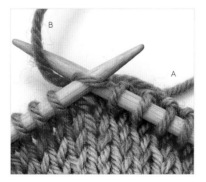

STEP 1
To work a knit stitch in A, color B is woven in. Insert the right needle to begin a knit stitch as normal. Take B around the left needle as if to begin a knit stitch.

STEP 2
Wrap A around the right needle as if to begin a knit stitch. Both A and B are around the right needle at this point.

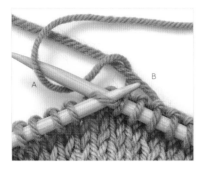

STEP 3
Before completing the stitch, bring B back around the right needle (i.e., reversing step 1.). Note how B now lays over A. Leaving B in this position, complete the knit stitch with A.

STEP 4
If the next stitches are worked in A, work two stitches, then repeat steps 1–3. If not, change to B, bringing B up from under A. The yarns should not be twisted at this point.

WEAVING IN ON A PURL ROW

STEP 1
To work a purl stitch in A, color B is woven in. Insert the right needle into the stitch purlwise as normal. Wrap B around the right needle as if to purl.

STEP 2
Bringing A up from under B, wrap A around the right needle as if to purl.

STEP 3
Bring B back around the right needle so A lays across the front of B. Complete the purl stitch in A.

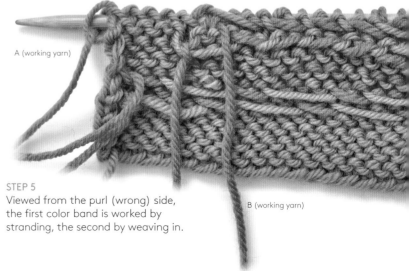

A (working yarn)

B (working yarn)

STEP 4
Bring B back around the right needle so A lays across the front of B, ready to purl the next stitch in A.

STEP 5
Viewed from the purl (wrong) side, the first color band is worked by stranding, the second by weaving in.

WORKING WITH ONE YARN IN EACH HAND

This method combines the U.S./Continental European left-handed style of knitting and the right-handed British style. One yarn is held in each hand and both are used in the same row. This technique takes practice, but once you've mastered it, you will never look back!

TWO-HANDED STRANDING ON A KNIT ROW

STEP 1
Knit with color A in the right hand and B in the left hand. Keep B evenly gauged and out of the way of the stitch about to be worked. When the first color change is reached, don't break off color A. Leaving a 4in. (10cm) tail of color B, hold A and B together and knot color B to color A, as close to the edge of the work as possible, but not too tight as you will undo this later.

STEP 2
Knit the new stitch using color B, knitting U.S./Continental style.

STEP 3
Note how the yarns are anchored, but with one yarn in either hand they are not twisted.

STEP 4
At the next color change, bring color A over color B. Continuing to hold A to the left, knit in color A, using the right hand to manipulate the yarn (UK style).

STEP 5
Again, note how the yarns are anchored, but with one yarn in either hand they are not twisted.

STEP 6
Repeat at each color change until the end of the row. Using this method you should find that the stitches are all safely anchored in place, but the yarns are not tangled at the back and are ready to move onto the next row.

TWO-HANDED STRANDING ON A PURL ROW

STEP 1
As with knit rows, working with color A in your right hand, use the right hand to manipulate the yarn (UK style), until you reach the color change. Bring color B up under A to create the anchor.

STEP 2
Purl the next stitch in color B, holding the yarn in your left hand and purling U.S./Continental style.

STEP 3
Note how the yarns are anchored, but with one yarn in either hand they are not twisted.

STEP 4
Repeat at each color change until the end of the row. Using this method you should find that the yarns do not tangle at the back.

TWO-HANDED WEAVING IN ON A KNIT ROW (WEAVE IN COLOR A OR B)

STEP 1
To weave in color B on a knit row (color B is in the left hand), insert the tip of the right needle into the next stitch knitwise. The right needle then continues below color B, going from front to back.

STEP 2
Wrap color A around the needle as if to knit.

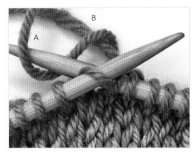

STEP 3
Before completing the knit stitch, take color B back around the right needle. Color B crosses over and is caught in place by color A.

STEP 4
Complete the stitch and, if continuing in color A, knit two more stitches, then repeat steps 1–3. If continuing in color B, bring up color B from underneath A and continue to knit in A.

STEP 5
Repeat to the end of the row, weaving in wherever there are more than three stitches in a given color between color changes.

 ## TOP TIPS FOR SUCCESSFUL COLORWAYS

It can be difficult to work out which colors go together in a colorwork design. Here are a few ideas to get you started.

- Using a favorite photograph, picture, or magazine illustration can inspire a very pleasing combination of colors.

- Invest in a color wheel. If you don't have one, there are many free printable ones available on the internet. Choose your main colors from a color family, for example, pinks/blue/purples sit next to each other on the color wheel. Then pick an accent color from the opposite side of the color wheel. For example, yellow sits opposite purple and green sits opposite red. This will make your design really pop.

- Think about proportion as well as the actual colors. The accent color will be quite dominant, so choose a part of the design with a smaller number of stitches to ensure that it doesn't overwhelm the rest of the pattern.

- Choose your background color carefully. A neutral ecru or cream will work with many colorways, but others can be really different and effective. Have a look at other patterns and images online for more ideas.

TWO-HANDED WEAVING IN ON A PURL ROW (WEAVE IN COLOR A)
On purl rows, to weave in the yarn in your left hand (A), proceed as follows.

STEP 1
To weave in the yarn (A) in your left hand on a purl row, purl two stitches in yarn A. To anchor the first point where you need to weave in, wrap the yarns together and hold A to the left.

STEP 2
Wrap color A around the right needle counterclockwise. Wrap color B around the needle, also counterclockwise, but, before completing the stitch in B, take color A back around the right needle (undoing the wrap you just made with A). Color B lays over color A.

STEP 3
Complete the purl stitch in color B.

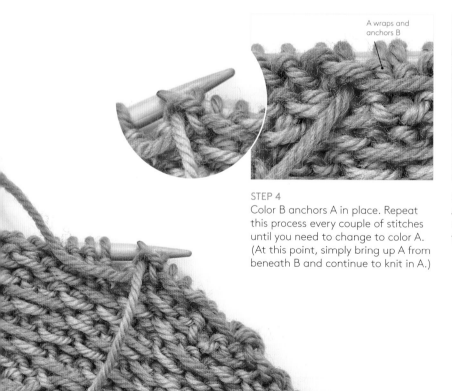

A wraps and anchors B

STEP 4
Color B anchors A in place. Repeat this process every couple of stitches until you need to change to color A. (At this point, simply bring up A from beneath B and continue to knit in A.)

STEP 5
At the end of the row, the yarns remain one in either hand and the yarn is secure but not tangled.

TWO-HANDED WEAVING IN ON A PURL ROW (WEAVE IN COLOR B)
On purl rows, to weave in the yarn in your right hand (B), proceed as follows.

STEP 1
To weave in color B when it is in your right hand on a purl row, purl two stitches in B. Insert the tip of the right needle into the next stitch and wrap color B around the right needle clockwise (i.e., in the opposite direction to normal).

STEP 2
Wrap color A around the needle purlwise as normal, but, before completing the stitch, take A clockwise back around the needle. Yarn B is secured below yarn A.

STEP 3
Complete the purl stitch in color A.

STEP 4
At the end of the row, the yarns remain one in either hand and the yarn is secure but not tangled.

CLINIC

I THOUGHT I'D CHOSEN A GOOD SELECTION OF COLORS, BUT THE PATTERN DOESN'T REALLY STAND OUT. WHAT COULD I HAVE DONE TO MAKE THE COLORS MORE VIBRANT?

If your pattern is disappearing against the background, you may just need to select a different background color. A heathered, soft shade can be very effective behind a set of solid colors, even if it is from a similar color family. Have a look at other patterns and images online for more ideas.

Naturally, you don't want to buy lots of yarn that you might not need, so here's my top tip:

Ask the yarn store if you can take a black-and-white photo of your colors. If you explain why, they shouldn't mind. Line the colors up in the order you are thinking of using them in the pattern and include a ball of the background yarn. Is there a good variation in shade, as in the example shown right, or do they all look "mid-gray"? There should be some good variation in light and shade for a good colorway. Here, the dark colors are very similar in tone, so try not to have them next to one another in the pattern or they may blend into one another. Once you have your set of colors, try different ways of combining them and make swatches to test how they look.

Intarsia colorwork

Intarsia is a neat way to create blocks of
color where stranding or weaving in (see
pages 112–121) would look unsightly
and be unnecessarily cumbersome.

INTARSIA VERSUS STRANDING

Intarsia is particularly popular for picture knitting,
where a design is worked in a single area (for
example, a large motif on the front of a sweater);
however, small motifs placed more widely apart
may also be best worked in intarsia.

There are several advantages to using intarsia
over stranding or weaving in. With intarsia there
are no strands at the back of the work to snag or
catch. Stranding makes a fabric heavier and
thicker, which may not always be desirable,
particularly on garments where drape, give, or soft
textures are needed. Light-colored main fabrics,
finer yarns, and open textures may allow stranded
yarns to be seen, spoiling the overall effect.

HOW DOES INTARSIA WORK?

Unlike Fair Isle knitting, where yarns not in use
are carried along at the back of the work, intarsia
simply uses a separate bobbin/ball of yarn for each
section of color. One might expect this to result in
a tangled mess of yarn. Fortunately, there are
numerous easy techniques you can use to keep
yarns under control.

These samples have been made in intarsia. Note
all the threads where each color has been made
using a separate butterfly of yarn—it is a lot to
weave in, but creates a much nicer finish when
seen from the front!

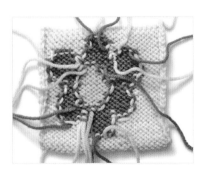

< Start point for motif and direction of knitting (in color A)	Odd rows knit, even rows purl
Odd rows knit, even rows purl	Odd rows knit, even rows purl

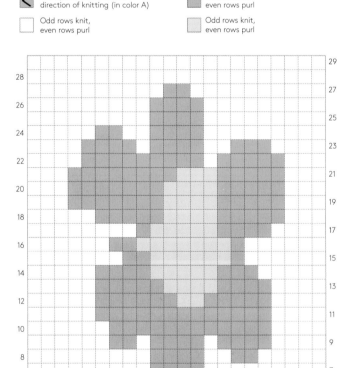

PREPARING YARN FOR KNITTING

If only a few stitches are to be worked in a particular color, rather than using a full-size ball, it is more convenient to wind a small amount onto a bobbin, a small piece of card, or into a "butterfly," as shown here. Estimating the amount of yarn needed improves with practice, and new yarn can always be joined in if you run out.

STEP 1
To make a butterfly, lay a 5in. (12.5cm) tail of yarn across your palm.

STEP 2
Wrap the yarn in a figure-eight around your thumb and little finger, holding the fingers about 3in. (7.5cm) apart.

STEP 3
When enough yarn has been wound, cut off the yarn, leaving a 5in. (12.5cm) tail. Leaving the loops on your fingers, pass the cut end up behind the loops.

STEP 4
Bring it forward over the loops and tuck it beneath the last wrap. Pull tight.

STEP 5
Remove the wrapped loops and draw off the yarn from the center tail (the end you didn't tie the butterfly with).

TOP TIPS FOR SUCCESSFUL INTARSIA KNITTING

- For just a few stitches in a particular color, simply cut a long strand of yarn and use that to knit small sections.

- Prevent butterflies from tangling by only unwinding yarn as needed. This also reduces strain on the yarn, keeping the gauge even.

- Weaving in ends as you go makes the process seem less daunting than leaving them all until the end.

MAKING AN INTARSIA MOTIF

Whether you are sprinkling small motifs across a sweater or creating a much larger image, the techniques for intarsia are essentially the same.

STEP 1
Knit in color A to the color change. Leave a tail of 4–5in. (10–12.5cm) of the new yarn (color B) at the back of the work to sew in later. You may find it easier to loosely knot color B around color A to stop the stitches working loose. This will be undone later, so shouldn't be too tight.

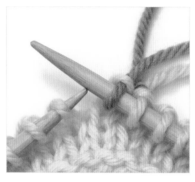

STEP 2
Make the next stitch in color B. Do not cut off color A, but leave it at the back of the work.

STEP 3
Hold color B firmly and knit in B until the next color is required. This may be color A or a new color altogether. At this stage, the first stitch may be a little loose. If necessary, pull the tail end gently, enough to stop the stitch raveling but not enough to pucker the knitting.

COLORWORK DETAILS

It's not necessary to create a garment entirely in colorwork. Try these ideas to add a little zing to your projects:

- Stripy cuffs, hems, and necklines are fun and funky.

- A band of colorwork around the yoke of a garment gives a stylish look.

- On an otherwise plain sweater, blanket, or cushion, add some small motifs in contrasting colors. You can design your own motifs with knitter's graph paper (or online knitting software).

- You can also use graph paper to design your own, unique colorwork patterns.

STEP 5
Turn and, leaving the butterflies at the front, purl the second row. For a new color, follow steps 1–3. To continue with a color from the previous row, twist the old and new yarns by holding both yarns at the front of the work and taking the new yarn from front to back beneath the old yarn. Draw up the old and new threads, as necessary, to keep the stitches even.

STEP 6
Continue in the appropriate color until the next color change, repeating step 2 for new colors and twisting the yarns where the color changes occur. Gently adjust the gauge if the stitches from the first row have become loose.

STEP 4
Repeat steps 1–3 at each color change to the end of the row. There will be several butterflies dangling behind the work, one for each color change. Even if a color is used more than once in the row, a separate butterfly is used. For large sections, it may be possible to keep the yarn on the ball.

STEP 7
To twist yarns on a knit row, take the new color over the current color and knit the next stitch in the new color. Draw up the two yarns carefully, not too tight but enough to prevent a hole. Repeat for each color change. For a new color on a knit row, follow steps 1–3.

STEP 8
To finish off, thread the tail onto a yarn needle and carefully weave in on the wrong side (see page 139). Where possible, to avoid threads showing through, weave into the same color stitches. Check the stitches are not distorted or too loose as you work.

WHAT YARN SHOULD I LOOK FOR WHEN WORKING COLORWORK?

For good pattern definition a fine Shetland wool yarn is traditionally used, being warm, light, and durable. Look for something that has a little grip (it should fuzz up a little and felt when rubbed together). Superwash yarns can be rather slippery and can prove a bit more challenging for the beginner as there is no texture to hold the stitches in place, and it can be difficult to maintain an even gauge.

Colored knitting
BE INSPIRED

1. TOLKIEN CARDIGAN
This richly patterned, longline jacket by Martin Storey makes a real statement. Continuing the pattern theme in a single color and changing the background gives the design a sense of unity while allowing the knitter to have fun with the vibrant background changes.

2. THACKREY SCARF
Accessories with little or no shaping are great projects to choose when moving onto your first colorwork. This great design by Martin Storey has a short pattern repeat, which means you'll soon build up a rhythm and produce a stunning scarf in no time!

3

3. AZURE WOODS CARDIGAN

This design by Varian Brandon is packed with interesting techniques and would make a perfect project for a more advanced knitter looking to broaden their knitting skills. It has lots of elegant touches, from the corrugated rib and top-down sleeves (picked up from the armhole edge and knit to the cuff). The design is also knit in the round and then steeked (cut) to create a cardigan style.

4. EASY FAIR ISLE LEGWARMERS

These striking legwarmers by Lynne Watterson are a great project for experimenting with the combination of knitting in the round and colorwork. Short bands of different patterns add variety and interest, and the simplicity of the single-color cuff and ankle frame the design.

5. FAIR ISLE CARDIGANS

These two charming designs by Sidsel J. Høivik illustrate how different the effects can be when working with varied color combinations. With all-over color, these two lovely patterns will require careful attention and would be great fun for a more experienced knitter. Worked in very different colorways, they illustrate perfectly how versatile colorwork can be.

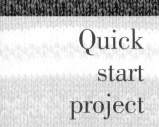

Quick start project

Fall-inspired pillow

This richly colored cushion looks complicated, but the pattern repeat is just four stitches. There are also resting rows with no colorwork, so you can take a breather! I've chosen strong colors, but this pattern could easily be worked in softer shades. It's also fun to try swapping out one of the colors for a variegated yarn, which creates a very interesting effect.

FINISHED SIZE
Finished cushion measures approximately:
13 x 13in. (34 x 34cm)

GAUGE
Yarn used knits as DK to this gauge:
20 sts and 24 rows = 4in. (10cm) square worked flat using size 6 (4mm) needles over stockinette stitch

YOU WILL NEED
• 2 x 4oz (100g) ball of DK weight yarn in color A
• 1 x 2oz (50g) ball of DK weight yarn in color B
• 1 x 2oz (50g) ball of DK weight yarn in color C
• 1 x 2oz (50g) ball of DK weight yarn in color D
• 1 x 2oz (50g) ball of DK weight yarn in color E
  (You will need approximately 880yd [800m] in total)
  Debbie knitted with Cascade 220 100% superwash wool DK,
  with approximately 220yd (200m) per ball, in the following five
  shades (although any DK yarn can be substituted):
  o Color A—Banana Cream (1915)
  o Color B—Pumpkin (822)
  o Color C—Lichen (867)
  o Color D—Blaze (1952)
  o Color E—Christmas Green (854)
• Pair of size 6 (4mm) knitting needles [or the size needed
  to achieve the correct gauge]
• Yarn needle (for sewing up)
• Cushion pad

ABBREVIATIONS AND TECHNIQUES
k: knit (see page 28)
p: purl (see page 30)
rep: repeat
RS: right side
st(s): stitch(es)
WS: wrong side
Weaving in (see pages 139–140)
Seaming (see pages 136–138)
Oversewing (see page 138)
Blocking (see page 141)

PATTERN NOTES
• The reverse of the cushion is made in two parts with an overlapping
  rib to hold the pad snugly in place. You could add a couple of snap
  fasteners under the flap if the rib becomes loose over time.

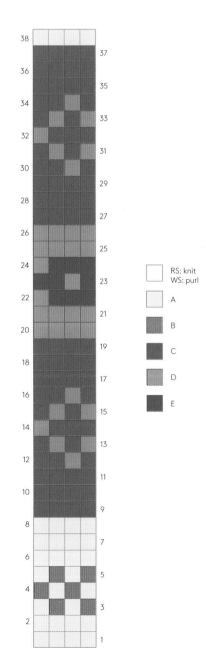

RS: knit
WS: purl

A

B

C

D

E

BODY
Front
Cast on 68 sts using color A and size 6 (4mm) needles.
Complete the front by following the chart, working the
complete chart (rows 1–38) twice, then rows 1–8.
Cast off, not too tightly.

Back (part one)
With RS facing and color A, pick up and knit 68 sts
along the cast-on edge of the front.
Row 1 (WS): Knit.
Row 2: Knit.
Row 3: Purl.
Rep rows 2–3 until the work from row 1 measures 6in.
(15cm), ending on a WS (purl) row.

Ribbed band
Row 1: *K2, p2; rep from * to end.
Rep row 1 until ribbed band measures 2in. (5cm).
Cast off, not too tightly, in rib.

Back (part two)
With RS facing and color A, pick up and knit 68 sts
along the cast-off edge of the front.
Continue and complete back part two as for back
part one.

TO FINISH
1. Before seaming, weave in any ends on the WS of the
   cushion. Carefully pin and steam block entire cushion.
2. With WS together, fold the back part one at the knit
   row. Pin the side seams in place and carefully stitch
   the side seams using mattress stitch (see page 136).
   Work on the RS as this makes it easier to see that the
   rows are correctly lined up.
3. Fasten off firmly with a couple of extra oversewing
   stitches. This prevents the edge becoming loose when
   putting in the cushion pad.
4. Again, with WS together, fold the back part two at
   the knit row. Pin the side seams in place and carefully
   stitch the side seams using mattress stitch. Work on
   the RS as this makes it easier to see that the rows are
   correctly lined up. When you reach the overlap section,
   stitch the rib and side together to form an overlap of
   the rib sections. This will be the cushion opening.
5. Fasten off firmly with a couple of extra oversewing
   stitches. This prevents the edge becoming loose when
   putting in the cushion pad.
6. Neatly weave in any remaining ends. Insert cushion
   pad and gently plump.

Guest Designer   Di Gilpin

My knitwear design studio has its origins in a semi-ruined croft on the Isle of Skye. I had settled there in 1983 with little more than a backpack containing a tent, wool, and knitting needles. From those early beginnings I have developed an international fashion brand, working with leading designers. We are now based at Comielaw Farm on the Balcaskie Estate, Fife, and have a showroom and design studio alongside a workroom for classes. We have a core specialist team of skilled home knitters, who live within a 15-mile (24-km) radius, to create the one-off pieces and special commissions desired by private clients, fashion designers, and the runway.

Colorwork mitts

Inspired by the abstract art of Sonia Delaunay and Sophie Taeuber-Arp, these mittens are playful with a contemporary colorwork design. Each mitten tells part of a story that is revealed when worn together. Knitted flat in intarsia with a gusset at the thumb.

FINISHED SIZE
Length: 10½in. (27cm)
Width: 4in. (10cm)
Thumb length: 4¼in. (11cm) from start of gusset

GAUGE
26sts and 38 rows = 4in. (10cm) square using size 3 (3.25mm) needles over stockinette stitch

YOU WILL NEED
• 1 x 2oz (50g) ball of DK lightweight yarn in color A
• 1 x 2oz (50g) ball of DK lightweight yarn in color B
• 1 x 2oz (50g) ball of DK lightweight yarn in color C
• 1 x 2oz (50g) ball of DK lightweight yarn in color D
(You will need approximately 800yd [700m] in total);
Di used Di Gilpin Lalland Lambswool, with 200yd (175m) per ball, in the following four shades:
  o Color A: Agate
  o Color B: Morion
  o Color C: Coral
  o Color D: Furze
• Pair of size 3 (3.25mm) knitting needles
• Pair of size 2 (3mm) needles
• Size 3 (3.25mm) double-pointed needle set

ABBREVIATIONS AND TECHNIQUES
beg: beginning
k: knit (see page 28)
k2tog: knit the next two stitches together (see page 41)
LH: left hand
M1L: Insert left needle from front to back under strand lying between the last and next stitch. Knit into the back of new loop, thus formed.
M1R: Insert left needle from back to front under the strand of yarn lying between the last and next stitch. Knit new loop formed, through the front.
p: purl (see page 30)
p2tog: purl two stitches together
RH: right hand
RS: right side
s1k1tblpsso: slip one stitch, knit one through back of loop, pass slipped stitch over without stretching it.
st(s): stitch(es)
tbl: through back of loop(s)
WS: wrong side
Seaming (see pages 136–138)
Weaving in (see pages 139–140)

PATTERN NOTES
• Each mitt has its own pattern and is knit on straight needles; the thumbs are knit in the round on DPNs.

RIGHT-HAND MITT
Cast on 52 sts using color D, size 2.5 (3mm) needles, and the long tail or thumb cast-on method (see pages 26–27). Continue in 1 x 1 rib as follows:
Row 1 (WS): *P1, k1 repeat from * to last 2 sts, p2.
Row 2 (RS): K2, *p1, k1 repeat from * to end of row.
Work rows 1 and 2 for a further 21 rows.
Change to size 3 (3.25mm) needles and colors A and B.

Continue working from chart 1 for RH. See designer's tip on page 132 for working from chart.
Row 1 is a RS row and also includes 2 increases at the end of the row as follows:
Knit 26 sts in color B, knit 24sts in color A, M1R, K1, M1L, k1. (54sts).
Continue working from chart in stockinette stitch and intarsia to row 16.
Row 17: Start of thumb gusset using M1R and M1L increases as marked on the chart.
Continue with gusset increases as shown to row 34 on chart. 6 increase rows worked and 12 sts made. (14 sts in total). Leave sts on a stitch holder to finish. At this point, stitches 53 and 54 are incorporated into the thumb and the chart continues as 52 sts.
Continue to row 70.

Row 71: Using color C, K2, s1k1tblpsso, k19, k2tog, k1, change to color D, k1, s1k1tblpsso, k19, k2tog, k2.
Row 72: Using color D, p2, p2tog, p17, p2togtbl, p1, change to color C, p1, p2tog, p17, p2togtbl, p2.

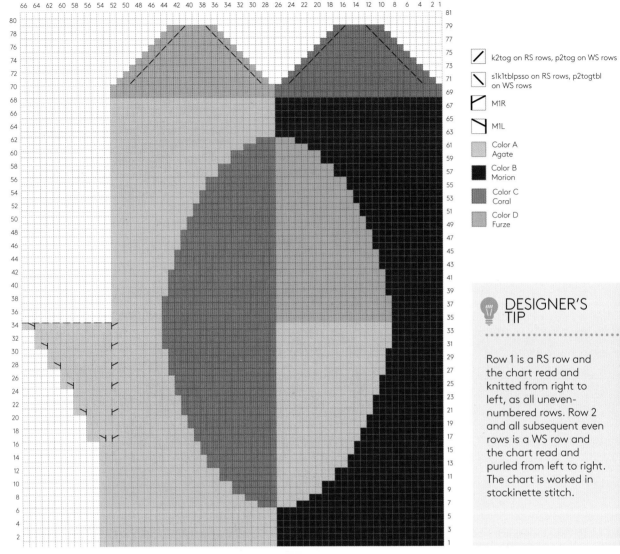

Key:

/	k2tog on RS rows, p2tog on WS rows
\	s1k1tblpsso on RS rows, p2togtbl on WS rows
M1R	M1R
M1L	M1L
Color A	Agate
Color B	Morion
Color C	Coral
Color D	Furze

RIGHT HAND

DESIGNER'S TIP

Row 1 is a RS row and the chart read and knitted from right to left, as all uneven-numbered rows. Row 2 and all subsequent even rows is a WS row and the chart read and purled from left to right. The chart is worked in stockinette stitch.

Continue to decrease on every row until you have a total of 16 sts, 8 of each color.
Work a 3-needle internal cast off as follows:
Divide the sts in half, putting the first 8 sts onto another needle (short, double-pointed). Place both RS together, cast off the two sets of stitches using a third needle.
Continue casting off across the 8 sts and neatly sew in the final end.

RIGHT THUMB

With RS facing, pick up and knit on the set of short, double-pointed needles the 14 sts from the thumb gusset in Color A. Cast on two more sts before joining to continue knitting in the round.
Increase two further sts on round 1. Total 18 sts across 3 needles.
Continue in rounds for a further 2in. (5cm).
1st decrease round: K1, k2tog; rep from * to end. (12sts)

Knit for 2 rounds.
2nd decrease round: k2tog 6 times. (6sts)
Final round: K2tog, 3 times.
Cut yarn and draw end through remaining 3 sts. Sew in ends.

LEFT-HAND MITT

Cast on 52 sts using color B, size 2.5 (3mm) needles, and the long tail or thumb cast-on method (see pages 26–27).
Continue in 1 x 1 rib, as follows:
Row 1 (WS): *P1, k1; repeat to last 2 sts, P2.
Row 2 (RS): *K2, *p1, k1 to end of row.
Work rows 1 and 2 for a further 21 rows.
Change to size 3 (3.25mm) needles and color A.

Continue working from chart 1 for LH. See designer's tip above for working from chart.

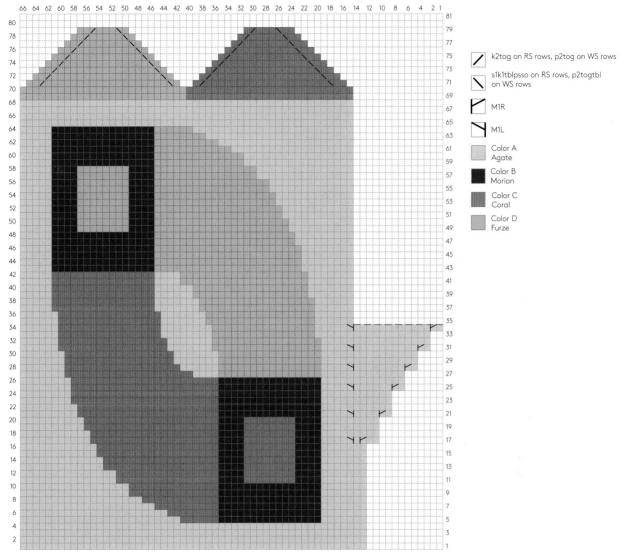

LEFT HAND

Row 1 is a RS row and also includes 2 increases at the beginning of the row, as follows:
K1, M1R, k1, M1L, k to end of row. (54 sts)
Continue working from chart in stockinette stitch and intarsia to row 16.

Row 17: Start of thumb gusset using M1R and M1L increases as marked on the chart.

Continue with gusset increases as shown on chart to row 34. 6 increase rows worked and 12 sts made. (14 sts in total). Leave sts on a stitch holder to finish. At this point, stitches 13 and 14 are incorporated into the thumb and the chart continues as 52 sts.

Continue to row 70.

Row 71: Using color C, k2, s1k1tblpsso, k19, k2tog, k1, change to color D, k1, s1k1tblpsso, k19, k2tog, k2.

Row 72: Using color D, p2, p2tog, p17, p2togtbl, p1, change to color C, p1, p2tog, p17, p2togtbl, p2.

Continue to decrease on every row until you have a total

of 16 sts, 8 of each color.

Work a 3-needle internal cast off, as follows:
Divide the sts in half, putting the first 8 sts onto another needle (short, double-pointed). Place both RS together, cast off the two sets of stitches using a third needle. Continue casting off across the 8 stitches and neatly sew in the final end.

LEFT THUMB

Transfer onto the set of short, double-pointed needles the 14 sts from the thumb gusset. Cast on 2 more sts before joining to continue knitting in the round.
Increase 2 further sts on round 1. Total 18 sts across 3 needles.
Work as for Right Thumb.

TO FINISH

Join seams from cuff to thumb using mattress stitch.

6
FINISHING TECHNIQUES

It is tempting, in your enthusiasm to complete a project, to rush the final making-up stage. To produce professionally finished knits, it is not necessary to learn a large number of techniques; however, spending a little time choosing the right seam, picking up a smooth neckline, and weaving in ends neatly will be time well spent. This chapter covers all these techniques and more to allow you to produce a garment to be proud of.

Seams

Knits can be joined using a very small repertoire of stitches. The key with seams lies in selecting the best one for the purpose. Factors to consider are the location of the seam, how much strain will be on the area when worn, and whether the fabric needs to be elastic or firm.

MATTRESS STITCH

Mattress stitch is an ideal seam for stockinette-stitch fabrics, particularly where long, straight edges are to be joined, because it is smooth, flat, and almost invisible. This type of seam is best for socks, baby clothes, and items worn next to the skin.

Use a blunt needle for this technique.

STEP 1
Cut a length of matching yarn of around 12in. (30cm), thread it onto a yarn needle, and run the yarn horizontally through five or six stitches along the wrong-side edge of the knitting. If you have a length of tail yarn to work with, use that instead and disregard this step.

Make the first stitch as near to the bottom corner of the work as possible.

STEP 2
With the right sides facing you and the Vs of the fabric running vertically, and starting from the bottom edge, bring up the yarn needle from the back and take the thread through a stitch on the left piece of knitting, as close to the corner of the work as possible.

STEP 3
Draw the yarn up. As you look at the knitting, the knit stitches run from right to left. If you look carefully, you will see a strand of yarn, almost hidden, at the base of the V of each stitch. Insert the yarn needle from right to left under this strand, on the right piece of fabric.

STEP 4
Draw the yarn up, but this time leave it a little loose. Take the yarn needle under the strand at the base of the V on the left piece of knitting.

STEP 5
Repeat steps 4 and 5 until five or six stitches have been worked. Draw up the yarn and the Vs should align to form a near-invisible join.

Draw up the yarn every five or six stitches and check the seam is smooth and flat.

STEP 6
Continue until the seam is complete. Finish with two small stitches, as per step 1. Cut the yarn, leaving a 6in. (15cm) tail for weaving in later.

BACKSTITCH

Backstitch is a good, all-rounder seaming stitch: strong and simple. It can be a little bulky in some circumstances, so is not suitable for delicate projects, but it is perfect for underarms, heavier garments, and housewares where a strong and durable seam is required.

STEP 1
Begin by placing the two pieces with right sides together (the wrong side is facing you). Run the thread horizontally along four or five stitches on the wrong-side edge of the knitting. Secure the yarn with two small stitches on top of one another. Take the needle through both layers of fabric to the back of the work.

STEP 2
Bring the needle through both layers of fabric to the front, coming out at A. Insert the needle through both pieces of knitting, taking it close to the corner (B). Bring the needle back up a short distance ahead of the first two securing stitches (C). This distance will determine the stitch size. For DK, stitches should be around 1/8–1/2in. (3–5mm) long.

STEP 3
Reinsert the needle at the end of the previous stitch (A), taking the needle from the front to the back and bringing it up at (D), 1/8–1/2in. (3–5mm) ahead of the last stitch (C).

STEP 4
Repeat step 3, each time taking the needle to the back of the work at the end of the previous stitch and bringing it up a short distance ahead of where the thread emerged at the end of the last stitch.

STEP 5
Take the yarn back down through the fabric at the end of the last stitch and bring it to the front again, close to where it entered.

STEP 6
When the seam has been completed make a couple of tiny stitches on top of one another, thread the yarn carefully back through the seam a little way, and fasten off.

OVERSEWING

This is a simple seaming technique. It does not produce a seam as strong as backstitch, but it is flatter and less bulky for areas that won't be subject to a lot of stretching and strain.

STEP 1
Place the two edges to be overcast with right sides together. Run the thread horizontally along four or five stitches.

STEP 2
Take the needle to the back of the work and secure the yarn at the start of the seam by sewing two small stitches on top of one another, through both thicknesses of the fabric. If you are right-handed, work from right to left. Left-handers may prefer to work left to right.

STEP 3
Take the needle through the edge thread of the back piece and bring it out through the edge stitch of the front piece as shown.

STEP 4
Take the thread over the seam edge and insert the needle in the back piece from back to front, going into the next edge thread along the seam edge. Bring it out through the edge stitch of the front piece, as shown.

STEP 5
Repeat step 4, working the stitches firmly but not so tightly as to pucker the work.

STEP 6
At the end of the seam, make a couple of tiny stitches, thread the yarn carefully back through the seam, and fasten off. From the right side (when worked in a matching color), this seam should be smooth and barely visible.

Weaving in ends

One of the main reasons for leaving long tails when starting and finishing with a particular color is to leave enough yarn to finish off neatly. Weaving in ends is neat and gives a secure but smooth and unobtrusive finish.

WEAVING IN ALONG A VERTICAL SEAM EDGE

STEP 1
Thread the yarn to be woven in onto a yarn needle. If it isn't already, take the yarn to the wrong side of the fabric. When weaving in ends along a side seam, take the needle through five or six stitches, working parallel to the seam edge.

STEP 2
Take the yarn under four or five stitches in the opposite direction, working close to, or through, the stitches just made.

STEP 3
Trim the tail close to the fabric, being careful not to cut the fabric itself.

WEAVING IN ALONG A HORIZONTAL SEAM EDGE

STEP 1
Thread the yarn to be woven in onto a yarn needle. If it isn't already, take the yarn to the wrong side of the fabric. When weaving in ends along a horizontal seam, take the needle through five or six stitches, working horizontally along the seam edge.

STEP 2
Take the yarn under four or five stitches in the opposite direction, working close to, or through, the stitches just made.

STEP 3
Trim the tail close to the fabric, being careful not to cut the fabric itself.

WEAVING IN MID-ROW

When I join new yarns, particularly in mid-row, I frequently begin by knotting the yarns together. However, this is a temporary knot that is undone later so the loose ends can be neatly woven in. Using this approach gives more flexibility, preventing stitches that are too loose or too tight.

STEP 1
Where a join has been made mid-row, the new and old ends may have been overlapped (I prefer a knot). Both types are woven in using the same process.

STEP 2
For a knotted version, carefully undo the original knot and join the yarns with a new single knot. This will allow you to reposition and adjust the tension and make sure there isn't a bump or hole at the join.

STEP 3
Draw up the single knot gently until it is more or less flat with the knit fabric.

STEP 4
Weave in the two loose ends, working in opposite directions to the direction of the yarn in the knitting. Working on the wrong side of the fabric, weave one yarn in to the right.

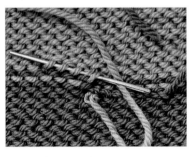

STEP 5
Weave in the second yarn to the left.

STEP 6
Weave the ends back on themselves for a couple of stitches, then trim close to the fabric.

 MAKING-UP TOP TIPS

- Choose a needle that is just big enough to thread the yarn onto and with a slightly blunt tip. For fine yarns, a tapestry needle is a good choice.
- Aim to go through the stitches rather than completely underneath them, as that will prevent the stitches being visible on the right side of the work.
- Leave long tails when casting on and finishing off. These are great for sewing up later as they prevent the need to attach a new piece of yarn in potentially vulnerable areas like the bottom-edge seam of a sweater or a cuff edge.
- Where possible, use the same yarn for making up as for the fabric. With very textured/fluffy yarns, use a yarn of a similar color in a similar weight to the main part of the yarn (i.e., the strand of yarn if it didn't have the fluff/slubs).

Blocking and finishing

Blocking (also called "dressing") evens out and enhances knit fabrics, restoring the knitting to its intended shape and size. Most knits will benefit from blocking and this is normally done as part of the making-up stage.

For blocking you will need a flat, clean surface into which you can stick pins and that won't be damaged by water/steam. Your bed or even a clean carpeted floor can be used, or clean fiberboard (covered with a clean sheet). Remember that there may be a couple of hours

drying time when you start blocking. Most knits can be wet blocked or steamed. For wet blocking, gently wash the piece and roll in a towel to remove excess water. Check the finished size measurements on your pattern and use this as your guide.

STEP 1
Using good-quality, fine, rust-proof dressmaking pins (you can buy special T-pins but normal dressmaker's pins will be fine), carefully pin the edges of the piece to the desired size and shape. Start with pins in the middle of each edge.

STEP 2
Next pin each corner. Ensure the edges are flat to the board, very slightly stretched but not pulled so as to distort the stitches.

STEP 3
Continue placing pins at regular intervals along each edge. Use plenty of pins to avoid distorting the fabric. Readjust the pins as required and recheck the measurements according to your pattern.

If the edge has points (on a shawl, for example), pin out each point. For wet blocking, simply leave the piece to dry. For steam blocking you will need to hold a steam iron or wallpaper steamer over the piece (do not touch the fabric and be careful to avoid scalding yourself). Keep the steamer moving over the fabric until it is damp, then let dry.

Picking up stitches

Picking up stitches allows knit edges to travel in a different direction to the main knitting. Contrasting yarns and interesting stitch combinations can also be incorporated into a picked-up edging, allowing designers to add stylish features and originality to an otherwise simple design.

Picked-up edges, when used as a base for fasteners such as buttonhole bands or cords, have a practical function because they give a garment extra stability, shape, or structure. Stitches may also be picked up around armholes in order to knit sleeves from the armhole to the cuff, along sock heel flaps, to create fingers in gloves, and more besides. Key features of a garment can be emphasized by the use of a picked-up edging.

Many knitters find picking up stitches particularly challenging and are often frustrated by the appearance of the edgings on their knits. However, there are some straightforward techniques that can solve this problem and, with a little practice, it is possible not only to achieve a great finish, but even to add customized edgings and finishes.

PICKING UP AND KNITTING ALONG A VERTICAL EDGE

The principles for picking up stitches along a vertical edge can be applied to most fabrics. Remember to allow for any adjustments you may have made to the length of a garment. If you have knit extra or fewer rows, you may well need to pick up more or fewer stitches than stated in the pattern.

STEP 1
To add an edging along the straight, vertical front edge of a garment, begin by measuring the edge and dividing it into manageable sections. Mark each end with a pin. Mark the halfway point between the two pins, dividing the edge into two sections. Repeat, dividing each section until the sections are about 4–6in. (10–15cm) apart.

Calculate the number of stitches to be picked up in each section by dividing the total number of stitches by the number of sections (in this case, four). Count the number of rows of knitting in each section to confirm whether a stitch will be picked up from each row (see Tip).

STEP 2
Holding the work in the left hand, with the right side facing you, start picking up stitches along the edge, beginning at the end nearest to you. With a knitting needle in your right hand, insert the needle under both "legs" (see opposite) of the second V-shaped stitch in from the side seam edge, on the first row of knitting.

STEP 3
We work one stitch in from the edge of the knitting because the very edge stitch may be loose and will give an uneven result. Keeping a tail of yarn about 8in. (20cm) long to the right, wrap the yarn around the needle as if to knit.

 TOP TIP

Often a stitch will be made into three out of every four rows rather than one per row. Too many stitches will make the band spread and flare out. Too few stitches will cause the band to pull in and pucker.

STEP 4
Draw the loop of yarn through the V-shaped stitch. One stitch picked up.

STEP 5
Insert the needle under both loops of the next V and wrap the working yarn around the needle, again as if to knit. Draw the loop through the V, allowing the loops of the V to drop off the needle.

STEP 6
Two stitches have now been picked up and knit.

STEP 7
Continue in this way, checking that the number of stitches picked up and knit in each section is the same as the number calculated in step 1. Note how the stitches picked up and knit follow a straight line along the next set of V-shapes. This is important if the edge is to look neat.

STEP 8
Once all the stitches have been picked up and knit, turn the work and continue working according to the pattern. If your work flares or puckers, it's well worth starting again, adjusting the stitch count (reduce the number of stitches if the work flares, add more if the work puckers or pulls in).

STEP 9
Viewed from the wrong side, you should see a neat, even edge with a slight ridge. Any ends can be woven in later (see page 139–140).

DID YOU KNOW?

Stitches are described as having two "legs." Imagine a person sitting astride a horse: the person's legs are the loop of yarn and the horse is the needle. One leg goes either side of the needle. The front leg is the half of the loop of yarn facing you; the back leg is the half of the loop going down behind the needle.

4 IDEAS FOR GREAT FINISHING

1   When you are picking up stitches, don't worry if you need a couple more or fewer stitches than the pattern. As long as it doesn't pull in or flare out, it will be fine. Remember to adjust the band pattern if needed – for example, checking that a rib still lines up.

2   Bands and edgings don't always need to match the main fabric. It can be fun to make a contrasting band or even use a different yarn altogether. You might even want to add this into the cuffs and hem. Just be sure to swatch first.

3   If your cast off is a bit tight, try the stretchy cast off (see page 45). If it is too loose, it may be possible to decrease a couple of stitches on the final row. This can look a little odd depending on the pattern, but can usually be hidden if the decreases are carefully placed. Try different options to see.

4   Don't be tempted to ignore picked-up stitches that aren't quite right. It may spoil all your hard work and it's much easier to take it back and re-try than to regret it whenever you wear the garment!

PICKING UP AND KNITTING UP A CURVE

When picking up around a curve (or going from a straight edge to a curve), use the same technique as for a straight edge (see page 142) but, as stitches are picked up, aim to pick up one stitch for each row of the knitting. If you hold the garment at an angle it is usually possible to follow the line of the rows and ensure that each row has a picked-up stitch.

STEP 1
Insert the tip of the right needle under both legs of the cast-off edge of the garment. Loop the working yarn around the right needle, leaving a tail of around 4in. (10cm) for weaving in later.

STEP 2
Draw the loop of yarn through to the front. One stitch picked up and knit.

STEP 3
Repeat this process, picking up and knitting one stitch for each straight row of knitting in the main garment.

STEP 4
Where the garment turns at right angles (usually where the bottom of the neckline is reached and the stitches go along the front neck), insert the needle under both legs of the V of the next stitch, one stitch in from the very edge.

STEP 5
Complete the stitch. Note how working one stitch in from the edge gives a much neater finish.

STEP 6
Continue around the curve, picking up a stitch one stitch in from the edge, so that it sits directly above each vertical line of stitches in the main body of the knitting.

STEP 7
To check, pull the fabric slightly straight and you should be able to see where the next stitch needs to be.

STEP 8
Work up the right-facing edge as for the straight edge, aiming to pick up and knit along the same line of stitches to maintain a neat edge.

STEP 9
When the neckline is complete, it should look smooth and nicely rounded at the curves.

PICKING UP AND KNITTING DOWN A CURVE

When picking up around a curve downward (or going from a straight edge to a curve), this essentially uses the same technique as for an upward-curved edge (see opposite). However, as the decreases on a left and right edge may use different decrease stitches, it can feel—and look—slightly different.

STEP 1
Insert the tip of the right needle under both legs of the top cast-off edge of the garment. Loop the working yarn around the right needle, leaving a tail of around 4in. (10cm) for weaving in later.

STEP 2
Draw the loop of yarn through to the front. One stitch picked up and knit.

STEP 3
Insert the needle under both legs of the V of the next stitch, one stitch in from the very edge.

STEP 4
Complete the stitch and continue to work down the left-facing edge as for a straight edge (see page 142), aiming to pick up and knit along the same line of stitches so as to maintain a neat edge.

STEP 5
Continue in this way until the garment turns at right angles (usually where the bottom of the neckline is reached and the stitches go along the front neck). Insert the needle under both legs of the V of the next stitch, one stitch in from the very edge.

STEP 6
Complete the stitch and work across the cast-off edge, picking up a stitch into the horizontal V of each cast-off stitch.

CLINIC

WHEN I'M PICKING UP STITCHES MY NECKLINES ALWAYS LOOK BUMPY AND UNEVEN. IS THERE ANYTHING I CAN DO TO MAKE THEM NEATER?

If you find it difficult to pick up the stitches with a knitting needle, use a small crochet hook to catch the loop of yarn behind the work and draw it through. Put each hooked loop onto the right needle.

When picking up and knitting with certain fabrics, it gives a smoother edge to work into the right leg of the stitch only. However, the stitch should still be picked up and knit one stitch in from the edge.

Once the stitches are all picked up, check for any holes or untidy edges.

Aim for a smooth transition from curve to straight edge, and check for gaps or puckering. It may be necessary to pick up an extra stitch or two on the turn, in order to prevent a hole. On the next row decrease to remove the extra stitch(es) and return the stitch count to the correct number. This technique may also be used at the shoulder when working a neckline.

Buttonholes

With so many beautiful buttons on the market, it goes without saying that the buttonhole should do the button justice by being equally beautifully made. If a buttonhole is noticed, it should only be because the knitter intended it to be so. There are numerous ways to make buttonholes, some more effective than others. A buttonhole should first and foremost be the right size: it should keep the garment fastened as desired and it shouldn't gape or sag. Buttonholes can be small and discreet or bold and decorative, and they may be clearly visible or concealed.

Before making any buttonholes it is a good idea to have in mind the buttons you will be using. It is usually preferable to purchase the buttons first and adapt the buttonholes to suit.

When choosing buttons, consider the size in relation to the project: chunky knits might look best with bold wood, ceramic, or glass buttons or even unusual materials like slate toggles. Fine knits and smaller projects may benefit from more delicate fasteners. Don't be afraid to go bold—strong contrasts or unusual shapes and materials can give a garment a real designer feel. Always buy at least a couple of extra buttons in case you need to adjust the spacing (or you lose one!).

The style and construction of buttonholes will vary depending on where the buttons are to be located. Classic cardigan or jacket buttonholes are set horizontally, often in a separately knit or sewn-on band. Buttonholes at cuffs, on pockets, and on waistbands may need different treatment.

HORIZONTAL BUTTONHOLE

This is a good, very neat buttonhole that can be adapted to suit the size of your buttons and gives a firm edge to prevent any sagging or looseness.

STEP 1
Knit to the point where the button is to be placed. Bring the yarn to the front of the work and slip the first stitch on the left needle purlwise (as if to purl) onto the right needle.

STEP 2
Take the yarn to the back of the work and slip the next stitch from the left needle to the right needle purlwise.

STEP 3
Using the tip of the left needle, lift the first slipped stitch over the second slipped stitch on the right needle. Drop the lifted stitch off the right needle.

STEP 4
With the yarn at the back of the work, slip the next stitch on the left needle purlwise onto the right needle.

STEP 5
Using the tip of the left needle, lift the first slipped stitch over the second slipped stitch on the right needle. Drop the lifted stitch off the right needle.

STEP 6
Repeat steps 4 and 5 until the number of stitches required for the buttonhole have been cast off.

This stitch moves from the RH back to the LH needle.

STEP 7
Using the tip of the left needle, slip the last stitch on the right needle back onto the left needle.

STEP 8
Turn the work. Cast on the same number of stitches as you bound off, using the cable cast-on method (see page 40).

STEP 9
Make an extra cable cast-on stitch but, before you place the stitch on the left needle, bring the yarn forward between the needles and hold to the front.

STEP 10
Turn the work. Take the yarn to the back of the work and slip the first stitch on the left needle knitwise onto the right needle.

STEP 11
Using the tip of the left needle, lift the last of the cast-on stitches over the slipped stitch on the right needle. Drop the lifted stitch off the right needle.

STEP 12
Continue knitting as usual.

CLINIC

HOW DO I DECIDE ON THE RIGHT BUTTONHOLE SIZE?

Make a small sample of the buttonhole band in the correct stitch. Place your button on top and count the number of stitches that the button spans. Most buttonholes will have the same number or one fewer stitches cast off than the width of the button. This may vary depending on the style of the button, particularly in the case of deep buttons or buttons with shanks. Experiment until you are pleased with the finished result.

Finishing techniques
BE INSPIRED

1. TILT CARDIGAN
A stylish turn-back collar and the addition of the buttons outside the edging band are interesting features of this design by Lisa Richardson. The pattern is knit in two yarn types in a rich Fair Isle, which lends an additional dimension. This is a pattern for a more experienced knitter.

2. GARDENIA CARDIGAN
The horizontal, ribbed button band on this cute cardigan by Linda Whaley would be a great project for the intermediate knitter to practice picking up stitches. The lacy hem and cuffs add a lovely delicate touch, too!

3. SWIFT DRESS
Knit in garter stitch, this is a stylish dress design by Lisa Richardson and is well within the reach of a beginner knitter. The interesting use of button fasteners at the shoulders gives it a quirky feel and, of course, pockets are always a bonus.

4. STRIPED SWEATER
Button-down shoulders are perfect for wriggly babies and toddlers, and they look smart, too. This sweater by Quail Studio would make a lovely project for a beginner to get started on simple finishings and easy stripes.

5. CABLED CARDIGAN
Such a bold design demands equally bold fasteners, and Marie Wallin has chosen crochet-covered buttons in a matching yarn. These make a statement without taking away from the elegance of the cardigan. The cropped length will sit nicely over skirts or trousers and is ideal for office to evening wear on a cool fall day.

Quick
start
project

Pagoda easy cable beanie

I call this the pagoda because the tiers and swirled points remind me of the exquisite designs of these magical towers. The cute cable on this slouchy beanie is stitched on at the end, giving you the chance to practice your cables and seaming techniques. The tiers of ribbing and a splash of color add a little something extra to this easy-to-knit beanie.

FINISHED SIZE
To fit approximate head circumference:
Small: 17¾in. (45cm)
Medium: 19½in. (50cm)
Large: 21½in. (55cm)

GAUGE
20 sts and 24 rows = 4in. (10cm) square worked flat using size 6 (4mm) needles over stockinette stitch

YOU WILL NEED
• 1 x 4oz (100g) ball of DK weight yarn in color A
• 1 x 2oz (50g) ball of DK weight yarn in color B
(You will need approximately 220yd/200m in total for the large size); Debbie knitted with Cascade 220 100% superwash wool DK, with approximately 220yd (200m) per ball, in the following two shades (although any DK yarn can be substituted):
  o Color A—Moss (841)
  o Color B— Peridot (286)
• Size 6 (4mm) x 5 double-pointed needle set (or the size needed to achieve the correct gauge)
• Size 6 (4mm) circular needle (or the size needed to achieve the correct gauge); the cord length may be 16in. (40cm) or 32in. (80cm) if working with magic loop (see page 92)
• Pair of size 6 (4mm) knitting needles (or the size needed to achieve the correct gauge) for the cable band
• 5 stitch markers (ideally with each maker in a different color)
• Yarn needle (for sewing up)
• Cable needle

ABBREVIATIONS AND TECHNIQUES
3/3 LC: 6-stitch left cable twist (see page 73); place next three stitches on cn needle and hold to front. Knit next three stitches. Knit three stitches from cn
cn: cable needle
DPN(s): double-pointed needle(s)
k: knit (see page 28)
k2tog: knit the next two stitches together (see page 41)
p: purl (see page 30)
rep: repeat
rnd(s): round(s)
RS: right side
st(s): stitch(es)
WS: wrong side
Weaving in (see page 139–140)
Seaming (see pages 136–138)
Oversewing (see page 138)

PATTERN NOTES
• The body of the hat is knit in the round. You may either knit on a circular needle using standard knitting in the round or the magic loop technique (see page 92). When there are too few stitches to knit comfortably on the circular needle, change to DPNs to finish the crown of the hat. Alternatively, use DPNs for the body of the hat throughout.

BODY

Cast on 90 (100: 110) sts using color A and size 6 (4mm) circular needle or DPNs.

Place a stitch marker on the needle and join the work into a circle, being careful not to twist the cast-on edge (see page 84–88).

Rnds 1–20 (RS): Knit every round, slipping the marker at the end of each round.

Rnds 21 and 22: Purl.

Rnd 23: Knit.

Change to color B.

Rnds 24–29: *K1, p1; rep from * to end.

Change to color A.

Rnds 30–31: Purl.

Rnd 32: Knit.

Rep rounds 1–32.

Next rnd: Slip marker, *k18 (20: 22) place marker; rep from * to last 18 (20: 22) sts, k to end. You should have 5 markers, evenly spaced around the circle.

DECREASE TO CROWN

Rnd 1: *K to 2 sts before marker, k2tog; rep from * to end of round. (5 sts decreased) [85 (95: 105) sts].

All sizes:

Rep rnd 1, decreasing 5 stitches at every rnd until 5 stitches remain.

Break off yarn, leaving a long tail, and thread the tail through the stitches on the needles. Draw up tightly. Fasten off by using a yarn needle to take the tail through the stitches and down through the center to the wrong side of the work.

(Note: If you are knitting on a circular needle, when the number of stitches is too small to continue comfortably on a circular needle, keeping the markers in place, transfer the stitches onto DPNs by knitting off one quarter of the stitches onto each DPN, then continuing as normal. You may not have the same number of stitches on each needle, but providing you keep the stitch markers in place, you will still be able to see where to make the decreases).

CABLE BAND

Using color B, cast on 18 sts.

Rows 1, 3, and 5 (RS): K3, p3, k6, p3, k3.

Row 2 (and all WS rows): K6, p6, k6.

Row 7: K3, p3, 3/3 LC, p3, k3.

Row 8: As row 2.

Rep rows 1–8, 15 (16: 17) more times.

Cast off, not too tightly.

TO FINISH

1. Fold the band in half and tuck the cast-on edge of the hat inside the folded band.

2. Pin the band in place so the two edges of the band enclose the cast-on edge evenly all around. The band should be very slightly stretched to give a snug fit, but without bunching or pulling in the body of the hat.

3. Carefully stitch the long edge of the cable band to the main body of the hat using small backstitches (see page 137). Stitch right through both sides of the band in the garter-stitch section. This will hide the stitches.

4. When the band is attached, neatly oversew the open ends of the band to each other.

5. Neatly weave in any ends.

Guest Designer Kate Heppell

By day, you'll find me working on magazines at Practical Publishing, where I'm the Editor of *Knit Now* and the Associate Publisher on *Crochet Now* and *Your Crochet and Knitting*. I get most of my knitting done on the move—I don't understand how anyone can sit on a train without yarn in their hands! I love to make simple, practical things and my magazine experience has trained me to write clear, concise patterns. My favorite yarn in the world is Shetland wool, but I'm not fussy—as long as I have sticks and string, I'm happy.

Clutch purse

This clutch uses a simple combination of knit and purl stitches to create a stylish waffle texture. With this pattern you will learn an easy technique to create buttonholes, so you can add a pop of color by adding buttons to your knits!

FINISHED SIZE
8¼ x 4½in. (21 x 11.5cm)

GAUGE
14 sts and 22 rows = 4in. (10cm) square using size 8 (5mm) needles over stockinette stitch

YOU WILL NEED
- 1 x 4oz (100g) ball of Chubbs Merino Super Chunky, with approximately 71yd (65m) per ball, in Pearl (RY71)
- Pair of size 8 (5mm) knitting needles
- 3 buttons
- Yarn needle with large eye suitable for bulky yarn (for sewing up)
- Optional: fat quarter of fabric, stiffening, needle and thread for lining

ABBREVIATIONS AND TECHNIQUES
k: knit (see page 28)
p: purl (see page 30)
ppso: pass previous stitch over
rep: repeat
RS: right side
st(s): stitch(es)
Cable cast on (see page 40)
Weaving in (see pages 139–140)
Blocking (see page 141)
Seaming (see pages 136–138)

PATTERN NOTES
- You can choose to work the stitch pattern from the chart or written instructions, whichever you prefer.

RS: knit
WS: purl

RS: purl
WS: knit

Repeat

PATTERN
Cast on 28 sts using size 8 (5mm) needles.
Row 1 (RS): *K4, p4; rep from * to last 4 sts, k4.
Row 2: *P4, k4; rep from * to last 4 sts, p4.
Rows 3 and 5: As row 1.
Rows 4 and 6: As row 2.
Rows 7, 9, and 11: As row 2.
Rows 8, 10, and 12: As row 1.
Rep these 12 rows 3 more times, then rows
1–8 once.
Buttonhole Row 1: P4, *k1, [k1, ppso] 4 times, p3; rep
from * to end.
Buttonhole Row 2: [K4, turn work, cast on 4 sts using
cable cast-on method, turn work] 3 times, k4.
Next row: As row 2.
Next row: As row 1.
Cast off.

TO FINISH
1. Weave in ends and block.
2. Lay work on a flat surface, with RS facing up.
3. Fold up the cast-on edge for four squares, so that the
   front and back are four squares tall and the flap is two
   squares tall. Join side seams.
4. Sew buttons opposite buttonholes.
5. If desired, add stiffening and lining.

Glossary

These pages feature technical words used in this book, along with some common knitting terms you might come across. Knitters have created their own unique terminology to describe some of the common features of knitting, and some of those words are also included here.

3-PLY, 4-PLY: Lightweight knitting yarns, sometimes called fingering.

ACRYLIC: Synthetic fiber.

ANGORA: Very soft yarn fiber made from the combed fur of the Angora rabbit, usually blended with other fibers.

ARAN-WEIGHT: Medium- to heavyweight yarn.

BACKSTITCH: Firm sewing stitch, also used to embroider fine lines and outlines.

BAMBOO: Fiber from the bamboo plant, used to make a smooth, silky yarn; also the woody stem, used to make knitting needles.

BINDING OFF: Fastening off stitches so they will not ravel.

BLOCK, BLOCKING: Treating a piece of knitting (by washing and/or pressing) to set its shape.

BOBBIN: Plastic or cardstock holder for a small amount of yarn.

BOUCLÉ YARN: Fancy yarn with a knobbly effect.

BULKY: Heavyweight yarn, sometimes called chunky.

BUTTON BAND OR BUTTON BORDER: Separate band, knitted sideways or lengthwise, to which buttons are sewn.

BUTTONHOLE BAND OR BUTTONHOLE BORDER: Separate band, knitted sideways or lengthwise, with buttonholes worked as knitting proceeds.

CABLE NEEDLE: Small double-pointed needle used to work cables.

CABLE: The crossing of two groups of stitches.

CASTING ON: Making new stitches on a needle.

CHENILLE: Type of yarn that makes a velvety texture when knitted.

CHUNKY: Heavyweight yarn, sometimes called bulky.

COTTON: Natural fiber from the cotton plant.

DECREASING: Working stitches together to reduce their number.

DE-STASH: Reducing your stash by selling, gifting, or swapping yarn.

DOUBLE KNITTING (DK): Medium-weight yarn.

DOUBLE-POINTED NEEDLE (DPN): Knitting needle with a point at each end.

DRAPE: Feel of yarn or knitting, and how it behaves in use.

DROP SHOULDER: Formed by a sleeve with a straight top edge, joined to a garment body with no armhole shapings.

DYE-LOT NUMBER: Indicates exact dye bath used, not just shade.

EASE: Difference between body measurement and actual garment measurement.

FAIR ISLE KNITTING: Small repeating patterns, knitted with two or more colors.

FELTING: Shrinking knitting to make a firm fabric.

FINGERING: Fine-weight yarn (similar to 3-ply and 4-ply).

FLAT SEAM: Method of joining knitted pieces.

FLOAT: Strand of yarn left at the wrong side of the work when stranding.

GARTER STITCH: Formed by working all stitches as knit on every row.

GAUGE: The number of stitches and rows to a given measurement.

HANK: Coil of yarn.

I-CORD (IDIOT CORD): Tubular knitted cord made with two double-pointed needles.

INCREASING: Making extra stitches.

INDIE DYER: Individual or small company that specializes in the production of hand-dyed yarn.

INTARSIA: Another name for picture knitting.

INVISIBLE SEAM: Seam stitched with ladder stitch.

KNITTING IN THE ROUND: Worked with a circular needle, or a set of double-pointed needles, to form a tube (also known as circular knitting).

KNITWISE: As when knitting a stitch.

LINEN: Natural fiber derived from the flax plant.

LUREX: Metallic fiber used to make yarn, either alone or blended with other fibers.

MATTRESS STITCH (ALSO KNOWN AS LADDER STITCH OR INVISIBLE SEAM): Neat method of joining knitted pieces.

METALLIC: Yarn or fiber with a metallic effect.

MOHAIR: Natural fiber, hair from the Angora goat.

NATURAL FIBER: Fiber naturally occurring as an animal or vegetable product.

NEEDLE GAUGE: Small gadget for checking the size of knitting needles.

PATTERN: Stitch pattern, or a set of instructions for making a garment.

POLYAMIDE: Synthetic fiber.

POLYESTER: Synthetic fiber.

PURLWISE: As when purling a stitch.

RAGLAN: Sleeve and armhole shaping that slopes from the armhole to the neck edge.

RAMIE: Fiber from the ramie plant, used to make a smooth yarn.

REVERSE STOCKINETTE STITCH: Stockinette stitch worked with the purl side as the right side.

RIB STITCHES OR RIBBING: Various combinations of knit and purl stitches, arranged to form vertical lines.

RIBBON YARN: Fancy yarn made from flat tape.

RIGHT AND LEFT (WHEN DESCRIBING PARTS OF A GARMENT): Describe where the garment part will be when worn, e.g. the right sleeve is worn on the right arm.

RIGHT SIDE: Side of the work that will be outside the garment when worn.

SEAM: Join made when two pieces of knitting are sewn together.

SEED STITCH: Stitch pattern with a dotted appearance.

SELVAGE STITCH: First or last stitch(es) of a row worked in a different way to the rest of the row, to make a decorative edge, or a firm, neat edge for seaming.

SET-IN SLEEVE: Sleeve and armhole shaping where the armhole is curved to take a curved sleeve head.

SHAPING: Increasing or decreasing the number of stitches to form the shape required.

SHETLAND WOOL: Loosely spun sheep's wool from the Shetland Islands.

SHORT-ROW SHAPING: Working incomplete rows to shape the knitting.

SILK: Natural fiber from the cocoon of the silkworm.

SKEIN: Loosely wound coil of yarn or embroidery thread.

SLIP STITCH: Stitch slipped from one needle to the other without working into it.

SLUB YARN OR SLUBBY YARN: Yarn of uneven thickness.

SOFT COTTON: Heavyweight embroidery thread suitable for use on knitting.

SPORT-WEIGHT: Medium-weight yarn.

STASH: Yarn you haven't started knitting with yet, e.g. yarn you have plans for, yarn purchased on impulse, or yarn you've been given.

STITCH HOLDER: Device for holding stitches temporarily.

STITCH MARKER: Split ring of metal or plastic, slipped onto a knitted stitch to mark a position.

STOCKINETTE STITCH: Formed by working one row of knit stitches, one row of purl stitches and repeating these two rows.

STRANDING: Method of dealing with floats in two-color knitting.

SYNTHETIC FIBER: Manufactured fiber, not naturally occurring.

TAPESTRY NEEDLE: Sewing needle with a blunt tip and a large eye.

TWEED YARN: Yarn spun with flecks of contrasting colors, to resemble tweed fabric.

TWISTING: Method of dealing with floats in two-color knitting.

UFO—UNFINISHED OBJECT: A project that hasn't been finished, and isn't likely to be in the near future. This is a likely candidate for repurposing. Knitters also like to discuss the number of UFOs they may have at any one time.

VISCOSE RAYON: Man-made fiber derived from cellulose.

WEAVING: Method of dealing with floats in two-color knitting.

WIP—WORK IN PROGRESS: Any project you haven't finished, or have recently (or not so recently) started. Knitters often refer to the number of WIPs they have on the go at any one time.

WOOL: Natural fiber from the coat of sheep.

WORSTED: Medium-weight yarn.

WRONG SIDE: Side of the work that will be inside the garment when worn.

YARN BOMBING: Public event where knitters promote their craft or a topical subject by decorating public places with knitting.

YOKE: Neck and shoulder area of a garment, especially where this is made all in one piece.

Resources

On this page are some indispensable conversion charts and references to help you along your knitting journey.

MEASUREMENTS

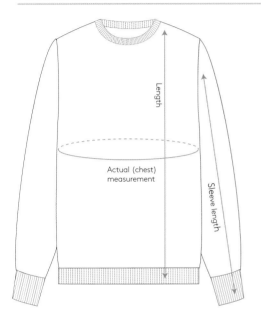

Length

Actual (chest) measurement

Sleeve length

Sizing				
To fit bust/chest	32in. 81cm	34in. 86cm	36in. 92cm	38in. 97cm
Actual measurement	36in. 92cm	38in. 97cm	40in. 102cm	42in. 107cm
Length	20in. 50.2cm	22in. 56cm	23in. 58.5cm	23¹/₂in. 59.5cm
Sleeve length	16in. 40.5cm	17in. 43cm	17¹/₂in. 44.5cm	18in. 46cm

NEEDLES

Choosing the correct size (diameter) of needles is crucial to obtaining correct gauge. Needles are sized in the US from 0 to about 20, and in Europe from 2mm to 15mm or more. There is not an exact match between the two systems. You can use needles sized by either system, provided you check your gauge carefully.

Equivalent needle sizes			
US	Europe	US	Europe
0	2mm	9	5.5mm
1	2.75mm	10	6mm
2	2.75mm	10.5	6.5 or 7mm
3	3mm	11	8mm
4	3.25mm	13	9mm
5	3.5mm	15	10mm
6	4mm	17	12 or 13mm
7	4.5mm	20	15mm
8	5mm		

Index

Credits

Quarto would like to thank and acknowledge the yarn companies who gave us permission to reproduce their images in this book. Knitwear designers are identified in the captions accompanying their work.

www.knitrowan.com
Designs using Rowan yarns appear on pages: 48–49, 74–75, 98–99, 126–127, 148–149.

NOVITA
KNITS

www.novitaknits.com
Page 75: Silvia sweater photographed by Karoliina Jääskeläinen
Page 75: Cabled headband and mitten set photographed by Riikka Kantinkoski
Page 98: Fox socks photographed by Eero Kokko

Page 127: Fair Isle cardigans photographed by Anne Helene Gjelstad

SUPPLIER

With grateful thanks to Cascade for providing yarns used in the technical step-by-step sections and the Azure woods cardigan image on page 127.

www.cascadeyarns.com

Photographs on the "Be inspired" pages are used with permission of the yarn companies. All other images are the copyright of Quarto Publishing plc. While every effort has been made to credit contributors, Quarto would like to apologize should there have been any omissions or errors—and would be pleased to make the appropriate correction for future editions of the book.

AUTHOR CREDITS

My first thank you must go to my Granny; to the lady who took a risk on an awkward teenager, giving me my first knitting job; to the knitting magazines and of course to Quarto for putting their faith in my writing and designing; to my dear friend Julia who gently critiques and patiently test-knits my designs—she is my knitting rock; and, to my lovely family who put up with the constant clicking of needles and finding fuzzy balls of yarn stashed all over the house!